Your
BULL TERRIER

By Marilyn Drewes

Compiled and Edited by
William W. Denlinger and R. Annabel Rathman

Cover Design by
Bruce Parker

DENLINGER'S PUBLISHERS, LTD.
Box 76, Fairfax, Virginia 22030

This book is affectionately dedicated
to Dad
in appreciation for all his help
in raising and in caring for
Nippy's Bull Terriers

The Author, Marilyn Drewes, and five-month-old Nippy's Fan of Briarbrook, "Fanny," by Ch. Banbury Borealis ex Ch. Nippy's Silver Duchess.

Foreword

"Several millions of Englishmen, and for that matter Scotsmen, are unable to contemplate life without the company of a dog. Of these, a small, discriminating minority are unable to contemplate it without the company of a Bull Terrier"— Henry Longhurst, from *The Bull Terrier Book,* published by the Bull Terrier Club, England, 1954.

Although Henry Longhurst's words were written more than twenty years ago, it is still "a small, discriminating minority," whether in England or any other country, including the United States, who are addicted to the Bull Terrier breed. I say addicted because once you have grown to love a Bull Terrier, you are "hooked" for life. The question might well be asked then why, if the Bull Terrier is that wonderful, the breed is not more popular. I think there are several parts to the answer. First, the appearance of the dog does not appeal to everyone. Owners of White Bull Terriers soon become accustomed to such comments as, "Is that a pig or a dog?" or "What a peculiar looking dog. It looks like a sheep!" Second, the Bull Terrier has lots of character. He was bred to possess the strength and stubbornness of the Bulldog melded with the agility, intelligence, and impishness of the Terriers. An unmanageable fifty to sixty pound imp can be a problem. Thus, the Bull Terrier requires firm discipline. Yet he demands a great deal of affection and returns with interest all the love he receives. Third, it is an undeniable chapter in the breed history that the Bull Terrier was designed as a fighting dog. Today, most dogs are sweet tempered, but if provoked into a fight, the Bull Terrier will finish it, often with dire consequences to the loser. Therefore, the conscientious owner never forgets the potential power of his dog and so takes pains to avoid situations where trouble might begin. Thus, some people might not want to assume the responsibility of Bull Terrier ownership. Finally, there are many people who are interested in dogs but who know little or nothing about the wonderful attributes of the Bull Terrier. They think of him only as a "pit dog," not realizing what a friendly, companionable fellow he is or what a delightful personality he has.

By picking up this book, you have shown interest in the breed. The chapters which follow will tell you more about Bull Terriers and will attempt to answer questions you might have about this type of dog. Then perhaps you too will decide to join the small, discriminating minority of those who cannot contemplate life without a Bull Terrier.

I would like to thank the many breeders who returned the questionnaire and sent photographs for use in this book. I wish it were possible to include pictures of all their dogs! Many thanks also to Mr. Raymond Oppenheimer, Mrs. Margaret Sweeten, and Mr. Thomas Fall for supplying photographs of the English dogs. And last but not least, I certainly appreciate the help of my amateur photographer colleague, Tim Keefe, in preparing many of the pictures.

M.D.

Contents

Your Bull Terrier Puppy   7

Conformation in the Adult   15

Temperament, Intelligence, and Personality of the Bull
   Terrier   25

Grooming the Family Dog   33

"Bed and Board" for the Family Dog   37

Maintaining the Dog's Health   43

History of the Genus *Canis*   57

History of the Bull Terrier   65

Bull Terriers in England   73

Bull Terriers on Other Continents   87

The Silverwood Trophy Competition   91

Bull Terriers in Canada   105

Bull Terriers in the United States   111

  Bull Terriers on the West Coast   113

  Bull Terriers in the South   117

  Bull Terriers in the Midwest   119

  Bull Terriers in the East   122

Manners for the Family Dog   129

Show Competition   137

  Bench Shows   138

  Obedience Competition   143

Genetics   149

Breeding and Whelping   155

Ch. Briarbrook's Terrathustra at three and a half weeks. Owned by Marilynn Larkin.

Ch. Holcroft Queenie's Nippy Girl with puppy.

Your Bull Terrier Puppy

Once the decision has been made to purchase your Bull Terrier, the first step is to locate one or more reputable breeders. There are many reasons for buying your puppy directly from a breeder. Let's consider some of the advantages.

The breeder probably specializes in just Bull Terriers. He (or she) really knows the breed and is raising dogs as a hobby with the hope of improving the quality of his stock. He is not interested in quantity production of puppies for mass merchandising. Therefore, a puppy purchased from his kennel should be well bred. This means that the puppy's ancestors were probably dogs of good quality, better than average specimens of the breed. A well bred Bull Terrier puppy should mature into a typical adult with most of the characteristics expected in the breed.

In addition, because he has a small number of dogs, the hobby breeder should be able to give his animals excellent care. His stock should be well reared, and each puppy should have received a lot of individual attention, a very necessary factor in the development of a well adjusted dog. In each litter, the breeder is hoping for potential champions. He will probably want to keep his puppies three months or longer so that he has time to assess the show potential of each one. He is not trying to sell off his puppies at six weeks for a quick profit and to make room for yet another litter.

A final point to keep in mind is this—most breeders are truly interested in the welfare of their puppies. They will attempt to determine if the prospective buyer can provide a suitable home for a Bull Terrier. Don't be surprised if the breeder asks a lot of questions about the family and the environment to which his puppy is going. On the other hand, the breeder is in a position to answer questions about the breed and to give sound advice on rearing your puppy. If problems of any kind should arise after the puppy is sold, you can call the breeder expecting that he will still be interested and anxious to help if he can.

7

There are various ways you can locate a Bull Terrier breeder. One good method is to attend some dog shows where Bull Terriers are being shown. Watch the judging and talk to the people who are showing dogs. Some of these exhibitors may be breeders with puppies for sale. If not, they can tell you where they purchased their dog and whether they are satisfied with the dog and with the breeder. You will find most Bull Terrier owners to be very helpful in trying to put you in touch with a breeder. If there are no dog shows in your part of the country, or if there are no Bull Terriers being shown, then you may locate a breeder by either of the following approaches. One is to write The American Kennel Club, asking for the name and address of the Secretary of the Bull Terrier Club of America. The Secretary will be able to supply you with names of reputable breeders. The other thing you might do is to pick up a copy of a dog magazine such as *Purebred Dogs– American Kennel Gazette, Dog World,* or *Terrier Type,* all of which have sections containing classified ads where you can find Bull Terrier breeders. If you can't find one of these magazines on a news stand, perhaps you can borrow one from a dog fancier friend, or else visit your veterinarian, who undoubtedly has some of these periodicals in his waiting room.

If you locate a breeder locally, make an appointment to visit his kennel. Please don't drop in unannounced! The breeder will also appreciate being notified if for any reason you are unable to keep your appointment. Oftentimes the kennel is too distant to visit. Then you will have to conduct business by phone or by mail. In any event, first tell the breeder what you are looking for. Do you want a dog for show or as a pet? Although most show dogs live with their families as pets, don't tell the breeder that you want a dog just as a pet if you really want an animal to take to the shows. No breeder can guarantee that a puppy will be show quality, but at least he can see that you get a promising one if you are interested in showing. Breeders want their best puppies shown and will try to pick their best ones for show homes.

Because Bull Terriers come in two varieties, Colored and White, you should indicate whether you have a preference. Some kennels breed both varieties while others have only Whites. Also tell the breeder if you have a preference of one sex over the other.

Occasionally a litter of puppies may be advertised in the local newspaper. The puppies might be well bred and worth looking at. Oftentimes such litters are bred by people who own one female and

Nippy's Impertinence at five months.

A promising puppy with a beautiful front.   Nippy's Silver Duchess.

Cordova Navy Jack at nine weeks. Owned by James De Mangos.

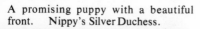

A good-looking puppy at about nine months of age.   Rocky C. of Holcroft.

decide to breed her. They probably won't know too much about picking the best puppies and they will be anxious to find homes for the litter since adequate facilities for keeping puppies for several months aren't available. Since you will most likely have to make the selection, here are a few suggestions as to what to look for and what to avoid in a puppy about two months of age. Look for:

1. A lively, plump puppy with clear eyes and a clean pink skin.

2. A short-backed puppy having a broad chest and sturdy straight legs.

3. A broad, fat rear end. When standing still, the stifle joint (the joint halfway down the hind leg) should be noticeably bent. It should not be perfectly straight.

4. A head with tiny eyes and the least hint of a stop. The stop is a depression in front of the eyes. It is characteristic of most dogs, but the Bull Terrier should not have any stop at all. Heads change so much that it is very difficult to predict what the adult head will be. Try to pick a puppy with a deep muzzle and as much bone as possible under the eyes.

The traits you should avoid are the opposite of the traits you want. For example:

1. Don't pick a sickly looking pup or one that cringes in a corner while its litter mates playfully tumble over each other or run over to greet you. A pup sitting off by himself calmly looking over the situation may be perfectly all right. A reserved pup is not necessarily a shy one, but if in doubt, pick the happy extrovert.

2. Don't pick a thin, long-legged, long-backed, long-tailed puppy. It may mature into a whippety looking Bull Terrier, hardly characteristic of the breed.

3. Try to avoid a puppy with large round eyes, an obvious stop, or a shallow, narrow muzzle. In a pet, the head qualities are not extremely important, but a successful show dog must have a good head. After all, it is the unique Bull Terrier head which sets the breed apart from all other dogs.

Other very important show qualities such as scissors bite, good ears, and good movement are difficult or impossible to judge at eight weeks. If the puppy's parents have good mouths, ears, and movement, then the puppy will probably be strong for these good features also.

When you drive to the kennel to pick up your puppy, be sure to bring a box or crate to put him in, particularly if you are alone. He

Eight-week-old Bull
Terrier puppy.

will travel more happily and safely in a sturdy container. At this
point I would like to say a few words about that wonderful inven-
tion, the dog crate. Novice dog owners are understandably reluctant to crate a puppy, for to them it seems confining and almost
cruel. I too felt that way. However, it doesn't take long to begin
to see the many advantages to be gained by accustoming your Bull
Terrier to his crate. Here is a partial list:

1. Traveling in your car, your dog is much safer in his crate than
he is jumping around from front seat to back seat. He is protected
in case of sudden stops or an accident.

2. For the very young puppy, the crate can serve as a playpen
when you don't want him under your feet. You can crate your
puppy when you leave the house, knowing that both he and your
household furnishings will be safe while you are gone.

3. Let your puppy sleep in his crate. He will soon learn to feel
secure and cozy in it. Even when very young, he will do his best

Ch. Holcroft Lady
Joan at six
months. Owned by
Alfred T. Bibby.

not to soil his bed. Thus the crate is very useful in housebreaking your pup.

4. If you decide to show your dog, a crate is a must. At a benched show, the crate fits right on the bench. Your dog has the security and safety of being in his own familiar "bed," and this certainly helps in settling him down amidst the noises and confusion of an indoor show. In addition, you know he can't fall off the bench and strangle on a bench chain, nor will he be pestered by passing visitors or by other dogs benched near him.

At an outdoor show, your Bull Terrier can remain safely in his crate while you watch the judging of other classes or breeds, visit with friends, or enjoy lunch with two free hands!

When you purchase your crate, be sure to get one that is big enough for an adult dog. He should be able to stand up in it, to turn around, and to stretch out full length. Therefore, check the dimensions and be sure that the crate you get is three feet long, eighteen to twenty-four inches wide, and about two feet high. If you are observant at the shows, you will see the various types of crates which other Bull Terrier fanciers are using. A useful addition for a wire crate is a canvas cover. Anyone with minimal sewing skill can make a cover by buying a few feet of canvas, draping it over the crate from the bottom of one side over the top to the bottom of the other side, and then sewing one panel for the back. The cover looks nice, makes the crate cozier, and keeps out drafts at the shows. Plastic or fiberglass crates are also very good and are usually best for shipping your dog.

In the case where your puppy is to be shipped by plane, ask the breeder to arrange an early morning flight, particularly in hot weather. Be certain to get the flight number, time of arrival, etc. Avoid shipping on weekends and over holidays. Try to meet the flight, although you can expect a delay in transferring freight to the freight terminal. Bring a choke collar and a lead so that you can let your puppy out of his crate to exercise and relieve himself. Never let a puppy or older dog out of his crate without first attaching his collar and lead.

Depending on his age, your puppy may or may not have had his permanent inoculations. Certainly he should have had his temporary ones. These inoculations rotect your puppy against the three most dangerous diseases of dogs: distemper, hepatitis, and leptospirosis. Be sure to check with the breeder as to what shots have been given. Within a day or two after getting your puppy home,

12

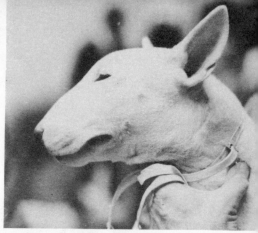

A lovely head. Tres Petite of Melrose after winning the Chicago Specialty at six months. Owned by Douglas K. Rose.

take him and a sample of his stool to your veterinarian. At that time he can have his permanent DHL inoculation if needed. Your veterinarian can check him over for general health and by testing the stool sample will determine whether treatment for worms is necessary.

There is one more important thing to attend to, and that is registering your puppy. At the time of purchase, the breeder will give you the puppy's pedigree. He will also give you the American Kennel Club form to fill in so that you can get your puppy registered. There is room at the top of this form where you fill in your first choice and alternate choice of names for your pup. If the puppy is older and has already been registered, he will have a name. However, you still have to fill in the transfer of ownership information. In either case, supply the information requested on the form you have and mail it along with the designated fee to The American Kennel Club.

Thirteen-week-old puppies owned by Marvin J. Tarlow.

Ch. Lavender's Robinhood, owned by Mary Andregg. Judge, Marilyn Drewes.

Conformation in the Adult

It was mentioned in the first chapter that Bull Terriers come in two varieties based on the dog's color. All white Bull Terriers belong to the White Variety. Any other color is classified as the Colored Variety. This artificial separation on the basis of color is necessary in the United States because dogs of the two different varieties cannot compete against each other in the classes at an AKC point show. They must be shown separately. Since both varieties are judged by the same Standard and since both White puppies and Colored puppies can occur in the same litter, they are quite clearly the same dog in every respect except color.

A White Bull Terrier is permitted to have colored markings anywhere on the head. In fact, head markings commonly occur in the form of eye patches and marks on the ears. Body marks from behind the ears to the tip of the tail also occur but much less frequently. Such patches of pigmentation are considered mismarks and are a serious fault. In the rare instances when they do occur, mismarks are usually found at the base of the tail, although they may occur anywhere. Some White strains have black or brownish specks in the coat. These specks, known as "ticks," are also considered a fault but are not as serious as a patch of color. Because ticks are pigmented hairs in the undercoat, a ticked dog will often have no ticks in the summer, only to have the ticks return when the undercoat grows in for the winter. The reddish-brown ticks usually disappear for good when the dog sheds its puppy coat. Black ticks, which are most likely brindle, tend to be more persistent and may reappear each year with the winter coat.

Several different colors occur in the Colored Variety. Brindle, though, is preferred. Usually the Coloreds have white markings on the legs, chest, neck, and head. A Colored with few or no white markings is termed "solid" for color. In addition to brindle, other colors seen in decreasing order of frequency are reds, fawns, tricolors, and black and tans. A Colored with too much white is disqualified from shows. The color must predominate.

15

In all other respects, both physically and temperamentally, the Colored and White Varieties are alike. When I described the separation into two varieties as "artificial," I was referring to the well known fact that all White Bull Terriers are actually Coloreds in which the color is more or less suppressed. I think I can explain the expression of color without becoming too technical, but if you know little or nothing about heredity, it would probably be helpful to first read the chapter on genetics further on in this book. The cells of a White dog contain two recessive genes, one inherited from each parent. We might label these genes "$s^w s^w$." These genes suppress the production of pigment in the coat except for head marks, ticks, and an occasional body mark. All Colored Bull Terriers have at least one dominant gene for color in each of their cells. This dominant gene, which we might label "S" or "s^i," allows the color to show. Coloreds with white markings probably have one recessive gene and carry either S or s^i and s^w. The "solid" Coloreds probably have no s^w, being of the SS or Ss^i genotype. In summary, then, a Bull Terrier may carry genes SS or Ss^i and be solid for color with little or no white; or he may carry genes Ss^w or $s^i s^w$ or $s^i s^i$ and be colored with white markings; or he may carry $s^w s^w$ genes and be white except for occasional markings on the head or elsewhere.

In breeding Bull Terriers, then, we could predict that two SS solids bred together should always produce solids while two $s^w s^w$ Whites bred together should always produce Whites. A solid bred to an $s^i s^w$ type Colored should produce all Colored puppies, some of which have white markings. A solid bred to a White will produce all Colored puppies with white markings. A Colored with white markings bred to another Colored with white markings can produce solids, Coloreds with white, and Whites. A Colored with white bred to a White should produce about fifty percent Colored puppies and fifty percent White puppies. Frequently, however, the expected ratios do not occur! Chance is always a very important factor in the actual proportions produced.

In addition to these genes controlling the expression of color, there are the color genes themselves. The inheritance of these is thought to follow the sequence: brindle, black brindle, red smut, fawn smut, clear red, clear fawn, tricolor, black and tan. Brindle, at the top of the list, is dominant to all the reds and fawns. Two brindles may produce any of the other colors, but two other colors (except black brindles or White carrying brindle) cannot produce brindle. The importance in knowing this is in realizing that the

16

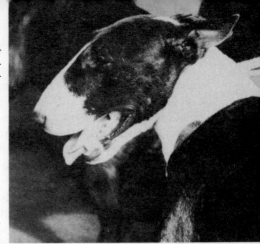

One of the best headed Coloreds ever bred in the United States. Ch. Midnight Melody, owned by Charles Fleming.

only way to breed brindle, the preferred color, is to make sure that one of the parents is brindle or a White carrying brindle. This is one reason why it is useful to know what color a White Bull Terrier is carrying.

One last question to consider before terminating the discussion of the two varieties is this: "Why is brindle the preferred color in Colored Bull Terriers?" A good Bull Terrier is a good Bull Terrier no matter what its color. Perhaps the founders of the Colored Variety realized that if ever the brindle factor were lost from the breed, it could not be regained without outcrossing to a brindle from some other breed. In those days, most breeders did not know that the Whites also carried genes for color. Now we know that a White carrying brindle can produce brindles when bred to any color other than White. The value of the brindle seems to lie not merely in the pleasing color pattern but also in the tendency for the brindle factor to be linked in some way with other desirable traits, primarily great substance. Most of the outstanding Bull Terriers in the breed's history have been brindles or Whites carrying brindle.

Ch. Papilio Pop Music, owned by David Merriam.

Whatever the color, however, remember that all Bull Terriers are judged by the same breed Standard. The Bull Terrier Standard tells us the characteristics of the perfect Bull Terrier. At a dog show, the judge compares the dogs in the ring with the breed Standard and places his winners according to how closely they fit the criteria for perfection. In actual practice, we find that some judges may interpret the Standard differently from other judges, or may disagree as to what parts of the Standard are most important. Let's take a look at the Standard for the ideal Bull Terrier. It will tell us what a perfect specimen of the breed should look like. If an animal does not fit the description given in the Standard, then the animal is faulty in that particular point. (The Standard is printed in smaller type. Following each section are my comments.)

The Bull Terrier must be strongly built, muscular, symmetrical, and active, with a keen, determined, and intelligent expression, full of fire but of sweet disposition and amenable to discipline.

This opening statement of the Standard summarizes the two basic characteristics of the Bull Terrier: his general appearance and his disposition. We must always keep in mind the purpose for which this breed was developed—to fight other dogs and to win. As much as we all abhor even the thought of dog fighting, the Bull Terrier must still look muscular and powerful enough to hold his own in battle. Certainly he should be a spirited dog, yet good natured, affectionate, and friendly. But because of his unusual strength, he must be able to learn basic good manners and he must respond willingly to his owner's commands so that he is always under control.

The head should be long, strong, and deep right to the end of the muzzle, but not coarse. Full face it should be oval in outline and be filled completely up, giving an impression of fullness with a surface devoid of hollows or indentations, i.e. egg shaped. In profile it should curve gently downwards from the top of the skull to the tip of the nose. The forehead should be flat across from ear to ear. The distance from the tip of the nose to the eyes should be perceptibly greater than from the eyes to the top of the skull. The underjaw should be deep and well defined.

The one feature which clearly separates the Bull Terrier from any other breed is the unique appearance of the head. People who do not know the breed may comment on how large the head seems. A good substantial dog can, however, carry this long, heavy head proudly and the whole animal will look well balanced. The arc which the head presents in profile is termed "downface." There should not be any stop where the muzzle meets the skull. To accentuate the downward curve of the head, even the tip of the nose

Excellent body with great substance. Doonhamer's Maximillion at fifteen months. Sire of Ch. Tantrum's Trad Lad. Owned by Philip Hyde.

should seem to bend down a bit, a desirable feature described as "Roman finish." Also in the profile view it is easy to see if the muzzle is deep and therefore strong or if it appears shallow or snipey and therefore weak. There must be an obvious underjaw giving the muzzle a rectangular or "square" look rather than a shark-like appearance. A dog with a weak muzzle and underjaw lacks biting and gripping power. In the full face view, the most critical feature is eye placement. When the eye is set properly high on the head, the desirable long foreface is achieved. A good head is completely filled with bone. This means that there are no hollows under the eyes and that the muzzle is not noticeably narrower than the part of the skull in which the eyes are set. There are very few dogs with well filled heads, for it apears to be easier to breed downface than to breed fill, and to breed both in the same animal is very difficult indeed. Of the two head characteristics, fill is more important because it adds strength to the head.

The lips should be clean and tight.

The upper lip should not hide the lower jaw. A pendulous lip would be a disadvantage in a fight.

The teeth should meet in either a level or a scissors bite. In the scissors bite, the upper teeth should fit in front of and closely against the lower teeth, and they should be sound, strong, and perfectly regular.

A lovely head. Ch. Nippy's Silver Duchess.

In the level mouth, the teeth meet edge to edge, resulting in a nipping action. The scissors bite produces a shearing action. Although the Standard states no preference, many breeders prefer a scissors bite, feeling that it is just a little farther removed from the undershot mouth than is the level bite. As the underjaw grows, a level bite may become undershot. Most judges penalize an undershot mouth very heavily, for it is an easily discernible fault. Yet the Standard does not appear to attach any more importance to a correct mouth than to any of the other virtues it sets forth as desirable.

The ears should be small, thin, and placed close together. They should be capable of being held stiffly erect, when they should point upwards.

Good ears add immeasurably to good expression. Small, erect ears close-set on top of the skull impart a look of alertness and intelligence. Soft (floppy) ears or ears set on the side of the head like those of a donkey are obviously incorrect.

The eyes should be well sunken and as dark as possible, with a piercing glint and they should be small, triangular, and obliquely placed; set near together and high up on the dog's head. Blue eyes are a disqualification.

A beautiful head. English Ch. Agates Bismarck.

Little can be said to improve on this description. The correct eye, more than any other single feature, gives that "varminty" expression which is so desirable. The smaller the eyes, the better. They are deep set for protection. Although blue eyes are a disqualification, eye color is pretty much an esthetic feature. An eye so dark as to look black appears more sunken and may seem to have a more "piercing glint."

The nose should be black, with well developed nostrils bent downwards at the tip.

A large black nose adds a lot to the head, particularly in the Whites. The bent tip or Roman finish accentuates the downward curve of the foreface. In some strains of Whites, the nose may lack pigment and therefore have pink spots, an undesirable condition purely from an esthetic viewpoint.

The neck should be very muscular, long, arched, and clean, tapering from the shoulders to the head and it should be free from loose skin.

The Bull Terrier requires an arched, muscular neck in order to carry its heavy head proudly. A short neck makes a dog look dumpy or, I hesitate to use the term, "piggy." Dogs with good shoulders laid back at the correct angle usually have long, muscular, correctly set-on necks. A long, thin neck, called a "ewe neck," is completely out of character, for it makes the dog resemble a sheep.

The chest should be broad when viewed from front, and there should be great depth from withers to brisket, so that the latter is nearer the ground than the belly.

The broad chest gives a dog that solid, "no one is going to push me around" look. Viewed from the side, the brisket, or lowest part of the chest, should clearly drop below the elbows. The underline then curves gently upward to the belly.

The body should be well rounded with marked spring of rib, the back should be short and strong. The back ribs deep. Slightly arched over the loin. The shoulders should be strong and muscular but without heaviness. The shoulder blades should be wide and flat and there should be a very pronounced backward slope from the bottom edge of the blade to the top edge. Behind the shoulders there should be no slackness or dip at the withers. The underline from the brisket to the belly should form a graceful upward curve.

To a "doggy" person, this description is very clear. To a novice dog owner, there may be a few fuzzy points. "Spring of rib" refers to well rounded ribs. A Bull Terrier should not be flat sided. "Back ribs deep" means that the ribs extend way back so that there is just about one hand's width between the last rib and the thigh. Although a Bull Terrier should not have a roached back like a Bedlington, there should be a slight arch over the loin. In properly laid back shoulders, when looking at the dog from the side, a line dropped from the withers to the ground should pass well behind the elbow. If the line hits the elbow, the shoulders are probably set too high, a condition referred to as "upright in shoulder." A Bull Terrier's back should be short and straight. A sagging backline known as "dippy back" is a serious fault. Finally, the body should be shapely, as described in the Standard. Sausage-shaped bodies are not typical of the Bull Terrier.

The legs should be big-boned, but not to the point of coarseness; the forelegs should be of moderate length, perfectly straight, and the dog must stand firmly upon them. The elbows must turn neither in nor out, and the pasterns should be strong and upright. The hind legs should be parallel viewed from behind. The thighs very muscular with hocks well let down. Hind pasterns short and upright. The stifle joint should be well bent with a well developed second thigh.

Length of leg depends upon the size of the dog. Balance is the key. A dog with the correct leg length will look square. Short-legged dogs appear too Bulldoggy while long-legged ones tend to be rangy and lack substance. The front must be straight with no hint of bowlegs or loose elbows. Propulsion for the heavy body is provided by the hindquarters, which must be very muscular. The main push to move the dog forward comes from straightening the stifle joint, which must be well bent to begin with. Unfortunately, straight stifles are a common fault in the breed.

The feet round and compact with well-arched toes like a cat. The tail should be short, set on low, fine, and ideally should be carried horizontally. It should be thick where it joins the body, and should taper to a fine point.

The tail should not reach below the hocks. When properly set on and carried, the tail completes the series of curves which begin with the head, follow the arch of the neck, then sweep along the back over the loin down to the tip of the tail.

The coat should be short, flat, harsh to the touch and with a fine gloss. The dog's skin should fit tightly. The color is white though markings on the head are permissible. Any markings elsewhere on the coat are to be severely faulted. Skin pigmentation is not to be penalized.

It's important that a White Bull Terrier have good pigmentation. He is not supposed to be an albino! Dark eyes and black nose have already been specified. In many strains, there are numerous black skin spots which may show through the coat, particularly if the coat is thin. Such spots are acceptable. Occasionally, though, pigmented hairs appear in the undercoat. These are called "ticks" and are penalized, though not as severely as a mismark.

Movement. The dog shall move smoothly, covering the ground with free, easy strides, fore and hind legs should move parallel each to each when viewed from in front or behind. The forelegs reaching out well and the hind legs moving smoothly at the hip and flexing well at the stifle and hock. The dog should move compactly and in one piece but with a typical jaunty air that suggests agility and power.

22

Proper construction at both front and hind ends is essential for good movement. Upright shoulders, loose shoulders, "out at elbow," and weak pasterns are all faults in the front assembly which result in poor movement. A long, weak back, poorly developed thigh muscles, straight stifles, and hocks bending either in or out produce incorrect hind action. At the present time, very few Bull Terriers are really good movers.

Faults. Any departure from the foregoing points shall be considered a fault, and the seriousness of the fault shall be in exact proportion to its degree, i.e. a very crooked front is a very bad fault; a rather crooked front is a rather bad fault; and a slightly crooked front is a slight fault.

DISQUALIFICATION: Blue eyes.

It is not possible to find a faultless Bull Terrier. In selecting your dog, particularly if you are interested in breeding stock, look for really great virtues such as an outstanding head, great substance, shapely body, and good shoulders and hindquarters. Probably no dog will have all these virtues, but the dog you buy should have at least some of them.

The Standard for the Colored Variety is the same as for the White except for the sub-head "Color" which reads: Color. Any color other than white, or any color with white markings. Other things being equal, the preferred color is brindle. A dog which is predominantly white shall be disqualified.

Ch. Banbury Borealis, winner of 1973, 1974, and 1975 BTCA Specialties. Owned by Allan and Marie Gerst.

Can. and Am. Ch. Regina of Colostaurus, owned by Gail Gordon.

This Bull Terrier obviously is enjoying his bath.

Temperament, Intelligence, and Personality of the Bull Terrier

Although each Bull Terrier is very much an individual, there are certain behavioral characteristics which are typical of the breed. These mental traits contribute to those qualities we refer to as temperament, intelligence, and personality. For many years scientists have made various studies on the relative importance of heredity and environment in the development of mental qualities. Both factors undoubtedly interact to mold each unique personality. However, those qualities which we associate with "typical" Bull Terriers must be largely hereditary, for they are so specifically characteristic of these dogs. The environment which the owner provides certainly helps determine to what extent the inborn potential of each Bull Terrier develops.

The importance of correct breed temperament cannot be overemphasized. The most beautiful dog with near perfect conformation is a travesty of a Bull Terrier if it has a poor temperament. On the other hand, a rather plain dog which might never earn a point at a show but which has the wonderful temperament expected in the breed will provide many years of fun and companionship for his human family. The challenge for the breeder is to breed dogs with both beauty and good temperament. In drawing up the breed Standard, the founders of the Bull Terrier thought temperament important enough to describe it in the opening paragraph " . . . full of fire but of sweet disposition and amenable to discipline." A Bull Terrier with correct breed temperament is a good natured, friendly, fun loving fellow. He is probably very mischievous but he is never mean. With children, he is patient and reliable. His whole bearing denotes confidence in his ability to handle any situation. Therefore, he is outgoing and readily adaptable to change. As a watchdog he is superb. Most Bull Terriers today do seem to

25

Part of the North York Obedience Club Drill Team. Trev (Labrador Retriever), Gael (Bearded Collie), Chevy (Rough Collie), Duchess (Staffordshire Bull Terrier), and Satan (Bull Terrier).

have the correct breed temperament. This is due primarily to selection of good tempered breeding stock. Fortunately for the breed, some of the most influential English stud dogs behind almost all the leading dogs today had wonderful temperaments. These include the outstanding English Ch. Beechhouse Snow Vision and his great-grandson Ormandy Souperlative Bar Sinister.

Among Bull Terriers then, poor temperaments are the exception. When they do occur, the cause may be hereditary, for some strains within the breed may tend to produce a number of shy individuals with uncertain temperaments. A more likely cause, though, is mismanagement of the puppy and young adult. There are still a few people of medieval mentality who continue to encourage aggressiveness in a dog. Ownership of a nasty, aggressive dog, a threat to both animals and humans, apparently gives a boost to the ego of these strange individuals. The purchaser of the puppy exerts much influence on the temperament of the adult. Excessively harsh treatment and discipline may change a tail-wagging extrovert into a cowed fear-biter. In spite of his tough, rugged exterior, a Bull Terrier is very sensitive and affectionate. He thrives

Ch. Dreadnought's Krackton Kwick, CD, "Kipling," owned by Kim Harter.

Shiloh Silver Sixpence and friend.
Owned by J. G. Mullins.

on love, attention, and praise, which are just as important to his full mental development as the correct nutrients are to his physical growth. Anyone who is unwilling to invest an enormous amount of time, energy, and affection in his Bull Terrier should not own one. You simply cannot shut away a Bull Terrier in the basement, banish him to an outdoor kennel twenty-four hours a day, or (Heaven forfend!) chain him in the back yard without adversely affecting his disposition.

I dislike dwelling on bad temperaments because they are not common, but here is one final thought on the subject. A bad tempered dog of any breed is unpleasant. A bad tempered Bull Terrier is dangerous, for there is no other breed as powerful for its size. Many apparently bad tempered dogs placed in loving homes with sensible owners respond wonderfully to socialization and kindness. If no such home is available, it is much kinder to put the dog to sleep rather than to send it to a dog pound. The very real and ever-present danger exists that the unwanted Bull Terrier will fall into the hands of the dog fighting fraternity, a fate far worse than euthanasia.

Ch. Bejobos Merry Sunshine and Bejobos Double Trouble, owned by Bob and Betty Cole.

On the canine I.Q. scale, most Bull Terriers would qualify as "superior." Some are no doubt more gifted with gray matter than are others, but the extent to which their innate abilities develop is, I think, directly proportional to the amount of attention and companionship received from the human members of the household. A dog which is played with regularly, taken for rides, walks, and on other excursions, and is, in general, treated like a member of the family will amaze you with how much he understands. On those occasions when he may act a bit dull witted, it is probably in a situation where he knows perfectly well what he should do but simply prefers not to do it! Bull Terriers are often stubborn. They are seldom stupid. You may recall an episode from Sheila Burnford's story *The Incredible Journey* in which the boy Peter decides to train "Bodger" as a retriever. At first "Bodger" responds with alacrity retrieving an old glove thrown into the woods. Soon, however, he tires of the glove game and his retrieves become slower and less enthusiastic. Finally he fails to return at all and Peter finds him in the woods frantically burying the glove!

Many accounts are on record where a Bull Terrier recognized a dangerous situation in time to rescue someone from traffic, an approaching train, or drowning. A Bull Terrier in England, Romany Rock Bar, received an award from the RSPCA for finding a lost calf which had fallen into a water-filled ditch and for then summoning human assistance to rescue the helpless animal.

Increasing numbers of Bull Terrier owners are having a lot of fun and experiencing great satisfaction in training their dogs for obedience degrees. Recently a Bull Terrier, entered in a competition for Shetland Sheepdogs, which are highly regarded for their obedience work, managed to be the highest scoring dog in the match! There is no reason why a Bull Terrier cannot learn just about anything that any other dog can learn.

When Bull Terriers are blessed with sensible owners who administer the proper doses of firm discipline as needed but give much love and attention besides, the dogs have a chance to develop their characters fully, and what delightful characters they have! A Bull Terrier makes a wonderful companion, for he is never dull. If he finds *you* dull, he will quickly think up some deviltry to wake you up from your lethargy and brighten his day! Your dog will joyously accompany you whenever and wherever you'll take him. You'll find yourself talking to him, and although he can't comment on your remarks, he will look at you with such a

Belle Terre's Cloud
Nine and Tao.

wise expression, ears perfectly erect, sunken little eyes peering forth, and often wrinkling his brow in an oddly quizzical way, you are positive he understands exactly what you said.

To me, a Bull Terrier is beautiful. I enjoy just looking at the exquisite head, clean lines, and athletic, substantial body. But there are many other handsome breeds. It is the Bull Terrier personality which is so utterly captivating and unique. Sometimes the behavior of Bull Terriers is a bit peculiar! For instance, they often race full tilt around the yard or through the house in a perfectly mindless way as though they are just so excited to be alive and must release this excess energy. Perhaps they will dance around in circles as though tail chasing, making odd grunting noises during the performance. Other mannerisms are clownish and endearing. Many Bull Terriers "speak" a peculiar rumbling sort of language usually accompanied by a furiously thumping tail, flattened ears, and a silly puffing out of the lips. Bull Terriers have such expressive faces! One very lovable trait is their pose when sleeping, usually in an arm-chair, on the couch, or best yet, in your bed. Wherever your Bull Terrier decides to nap, he will first curl up so as to

Bartholemew and friend. Owned by Ingrid Ackerman.

become as small as possible, rest his head on one paw, and then safely tuck his long nose under the other paw. If you speak to him, he will probably open one slanty little eye to let you know he's not missing anything. These dogs are famous for rolling back one eye and for looking at you sideways in a most humorous and charming way!

Bull Terriers embody such an odd fusion of contrasting characteristics—toughness with gentleness, deviltry with innocence, cocky self-assurance with pathetic dependence. A wonderful example of true Bull Terrier character is Ch. Nippy's Steven The Sea Dog, my fifty-eight pound White male. Everyone who knows this dog loves him. He is a rugged, fearsome looking dog with tiny sunken eyes and the typical "varminty" Bull Terrier expression. A fantastic watchdog, his raised hackles and roaring bark would intimidate all but the foolhardy. Yet, after proper introductions, he is extremely friendly and ready to play with his new acquaintance. He is most affectionate, loving to be hugged and patted. When told what a lovely, clever boy he is, he will lay back his ears, grin foolishly, and make happy rumbling noises. Given the least encouragement, he will clamber up on your lap or snuggle cozily in your bed. When there are puppies in the house, Steven, completely fascinated, loves to play with them. He patiently lets them chew his ears and lips and crawl all over him. Sometimes he pins a puppy under a great paw or appears to be gnawing on a puppy leg, but the pups don't complain, keep coming back for more, and all seem to love their "Uncle Steven." At a dog show, Steven appeared to ignore the competition and would stand as unperturbed as the Sphinx in a ring full of barking, snarling dogs. He did, however, loathe the Weimaraner next door! This neighbor, "Smokey," teased Steven through the fence while Steven, in utter frustration, raced back and forth along the barrier hurling Bull Terrier curses across the wire. One day I had taken Steven in the car on a short errand, for he loves to ride and sits up like the co-pilot peering out the window. As we pulled into the driveway, who was there but "Smokey." I wrapped Steven's lead tightly around my hand, planning to shoo "Smokey" away and then quickly get Steven into the house. But when I opened the car door, silly "Smokey" poked his head in, and this was too much for Steven! The next thing I knew, I was on my knees (skinned!) in the driveway, still clutching the lead, while Steven, gripping "Smokey" by the loose skin at the side of his neck, was giving him a good shak-

Ch. Belle Terre's Bring Down at birthday party. (Note ball in mouth.) Owned by George Mueller and Bill Schmitz.

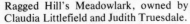

Ragged Hill's Meadowlark, owned by Claudia Littlefield and Judith Truesdale.

ing. I feared that would be the end of "Smokey," but suddenly Steven let go and "Smokey" scooted for home with no injury visible except to his pride.

Steven's dam, "Nippy," is a character in her own right. Although she has many idiosyncracies, one of the strangest is a passion for tunneling under the bedcovers. Sometime during the night she begins this mole-like burrowing, ending up at the foot of the bed. I used to fear she would smother, but almost twelve years later she seems none the worse for lack of oxygen.

Yet another distinct personality is Steven's sister Duchess. Exceptionally sweet, affectionate, and sensitive, she is also the resident hunter! Her specialty is moles, which she catches by rearing up on her hind legs and thumping down her front paws on top of the luckless creature scurrying under the leaves or snow. Each morning Duchy checks the birdseed barrel to see if perchance a mouse has fallen in. If one is there, she uses her front paws to tip the barrel toward her, reaches in her long muzzle, and snaps up the mouse. Bull Terriers are indeed wonderful characters.

Ch. Nippy's Steven
The Sea Dog.

Bill Syke's Bullseye, CD.   An obedient Bull Terrier.

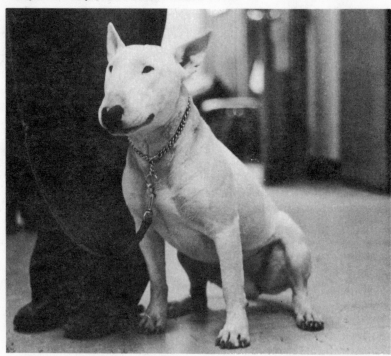

Grooming the Family Dog

Every dog should be taught from puppyhood that a grooming session is a time for business, not for play. He should be handled gently, though, for it is essential to avoid hurting him in any way. Grooming time should be pleasant for both dog and master.

A light, airy, pleasant place in which to work is desirable, and it is of the utmost importance that neither dog nor master be distracted by other dogs, cats, or people. Consequently, it is usually preferable that grooming be done indoors.

Before each session, the dog should be permitted to relieve himself. Once grooming is begun, it is important to avoid keeping the dog standing so long that he becomes tired. If a good deal of grooming is needed, it should be done in two or more short periods.

A sturdy grooming table is desirable. The dog should stand on the grooming table while the back and upper portions of his body are groomed, and lie on his side while underparts of his body are brushed, nails clipped, etc.

It is almost impossible to brush too much, and show dogs are often brushed for a full half hour a day, year round. If you cannot brush your dog every day, you should brush him a minimum of two or three times a week. Brushing removes loose skin particles and stimulates circulation, thereby improving condition of the skin. It also stimulates secretion of the natural skin oils that make the coat look healthy and beautiful.

Before brushing, any burs adhering to the coat, as well as matted hair, should be carefully removed, using the fingers and coarse toothed comb with a gentle, teasing motion to avoid tearing the coat. The coat should first be brushed lightly in the direction in which the hair grows. Next, it should be brushed in the opposite direction, a small portion at a time, making sure the bristles penetrate the hair to the skin, until the entire coat has been brushed thoroughly and all loose soil removed. Then the coat should be brushed in the direction the hair grows, until every hair is sleekly in place.

The dog that is kept well brushed needs bathing only rarely. Once or twice a year is usually enough. If it is necessary to bathe a puppy, extreme care must be exercised so that he will not become chilled. No dog should be bathed during cold weather and then permitted to go outside immediately. Whatever the weather, the dog should always be given a good run outdoors and permitted to relieve himself before he is bathed.

Various types of "dry baths" are available, and in general, they are quite satisfactory when circumstances are such that a bath in water is impractical. Dry shampoos are usually worked into the dog's coat thoroughly, then removed by towelling or brushing.

Before starting a water bath, the necessary equipment should be assembled. This includes a tub of appropriate size, preferably one that has a drain so that the water will not accumulate and the dog will not be kept standing in water throughout the bath. A rubber mat should be placed in the bottom of the tub to prevent the dog from slipping. A small hose with a spray nozzle—one that may be attached to the water faucet—is ideal for wetting and rinsing the coat, but if such equipment is not available, then a second tub or a large pail should be provided for bath and rinse water. A metal or plastic cup for dipping water, special dog shampoo, a small bottle of mineral or olive oil, and a supply of absorbent cotton should be placed nearby, as well as a supply of heavy towels, a wash cloth, and the dog's combs and brushes. Bath water and rinse water should be slightly warmer than lukewarm, but should not be hot.

To avoid accidentally getting water in the dog's ears, place a small amount of absorbent cotton in each. With the dog standing in the tub, wet his body by using the hose and spray nozzle or by using the cup to pour water over him. Take care to avoid wetting the head, and be careful to avoid getting water or shampoo in the eyes. (If you should accidentally do so, placing a few drops of mineral or olive oil in the inner corner of the eye will bring relief.) When the dog is thoroughly wet, put a small amount of shampoo on his back and work the lather into the coat with a gentle, squeezing action. Wash the entire body and then use the cup and container of water (or hose and spray nozzle) to rinse the dog thoroughly.

Dip the wash cloth into clean water, wring it out enough so it won't drip, then wash the dog's head, taking care to avoid the eyes. Remove the cotton from the dog's ears and sponge them gently, inside and out. Shampoo should never be used inside the ears, so if they are extremely soiled, sponge them clean with cotton saturated with mineral or olive oil. (Between baths, the ears should be cleaned frequently in the same way.)

Quickly wrap a towel around the dog, remove him from the tub, and towel him as dry as possible. To avoid getting an impromptu bath yourself, you must act quickly, for once he is out of the tub, the dog will instinctively shake himself.

While the hair is still slightly damp, use a clean comb or brush to remove any tangles. If the hair is allowed to dry first, it may be completely impossible to remove them.

So far as routine grooming is concerned, the dog's eyes require little attention. Some dogs have a slight accumulation of mucus in the corner of the eyes upon waking mornings. A salt solution (a teaspoon of table salt to one pint of warm, sterile water) can be sponged around the eyes to remove the stain. During grooming sessions it is well to inspect the eyes, since many breeds are prone to eye injury. Eye problems of a minor nature may be treated at home (see page 54), but it is imperative that any serious eye abnormality be called to the attention of the veterinarian immediately.

Feeding hard dog biscuits and hard bones helps to keep tooth surfaces clean. Slight discoloration may be readily removed by rubbing with a damp cloth dipped in salt or baking soda. The dog's head should be held firmly, the lips pulled apart gently, and the teeth rubbed lightly with the dampened cloth. Regular care usually keeps the teeth in good condition, but if tartar accumulates, it should be removed by a veterinarian.

If the dog doesn't keep his nails worn down through regular exercise on hard surfaces, they must be trimmed at intervals, for nails that are too long may cause the foot to spread and thus spoil the dog's gait. Neglected nails may even grow so long that they will grow into a circle and puncture the dog's skin. Nails can be cut easily with any of the various types of nail trimmers. The cut is made just outside the faintly pink bloodline that can be seen on white nails. In pigmented nails, the bloodline is not easily seen, so the cut should be made just outside the hooklike projection on the underside of the nails. A few downward strokes with a nail file will smooth the cut surface, and, once shortened, nails can be kept short by filing at regular intervals.

Care must be taken that nails are not cut too short, since blood vessels may be accidentally severed. Should you accidentally cut a nail so short that it bleeds, apply a mild antiseptic and keep the dog quiet until bleeding stops. Usually, only a few drops of blood will be lost. But once a dog's nails have been cut painfully short, he will usually object when his feet are handled.

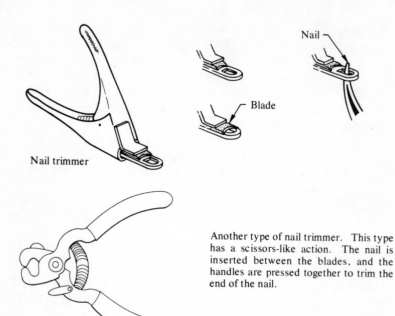

Nail trimmer

Nail

Blade

Another type of nail trimmer. This type has a scissors-like action. The nail is inserted between the blades, and the handles are pressed together to trim the end of the nail.

Dog crate with grooming-table top provides rigid, well supported surface on which to groom dog, and serves as indoor kennel for puppy or grown dog. Rubber matting provides non-slip surface. Dog's collar may be attached to adjustable arm.

Centered below is a grooming table with an adjustable arm to which the dog's collar may be attached. The adjustable arm at right below may be clamped to an ordinary table or other rigid surface which will serve as a grooming table.

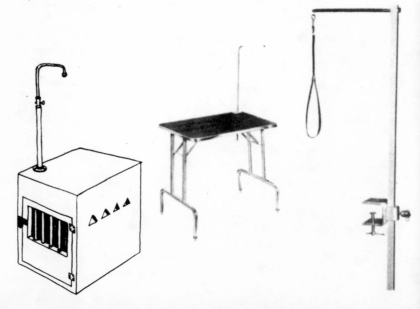

"Bed and Board" for the Family Dog

It is much easier to adapt to the demands of a new puppy if you collect the necessary equipment before you bring him home. You will need a water and food dish—preferably stainless steel and of a type that will not tip easily. You will need some chew toys, a soft puppy lead, and a soft hair brush for puppy grooming. You will need to decide where your dog is going to sleep and to prepare his bed.

Every dog should have a bed of his own, snug and warm, where he can retire undisturbed when he wishes to nap. And, especially with a small puppy, it is desirable to have the bed arranged so the dog can be securely confined at times, safe and contented. If the puppy is taught early in life to stay quietly in his box at night, or when the family is out, the habit will carry over into adulthood and will benefit both dog and master.

The dog should never be banished to a damp, cold basement, but should be quartered in an out-of-the-way corner close to the center of family activity. His bed can be an elaborate cushioned affair with electric warming pad, or simply a rectangular wooden box or heavy paper carton, cushioned with a clean cotton rug or towel. Actually, the latter is ideal for a new puppy, for it is snug, easy to clean, and expendable. A "door" can be cut on one side of the box for easy access, but it should be placed in such a way that the dog can still be confined when desirable.

The shipping crates used by professional handlers at dog shows make ideal indoor quarters. They are lightweight but strong, provide adequate air circulation, yet are snug and warm and easily cleaned. For the dog owner who takes his dog along when he travels, a dog crate is ideal, for the dog will willingly stay in his accustomed bed during long automobile trips, and the crate can be taken inside motels or hotels at night, making the dog a far more acceptable guest.

Dog crates are made of chromed metal or wood, and some have tops covered with a special rubber matting so they can be used as grooming tables. Anyone moderately handy with tools can construct a crate similar to the one illustrated on the opposite page.

37

Crates come in various sizes, to suit various breeds of dogs. For reasons of economy, the size selected for a puppy should be adequate for use when the dog is full grown. If the area seems too large when the puppy is small, a temporary cardboard partition can be installed to limit the area he occupies.

For the owner's convenience and to enhance the dog's sense of security, food and water dishes may be kept in the same general area where the crate is kept.

Nutrition

The main food elements required by dogs are proteins, fats, and carbohydrates. Vitamins A, B complex, D, and E are essential, as are ample amounts of calcium and iron. Nine other minerals are required in small amounts but are amply provided in almost any diet, so there is no need to be concerned about them.

The most important nutrient is protein and it must be provided every day of the dog's life, for it is essential for normal daily growth and replacement of body tissues burned up in daily activity. Preferred animal protein products are beef, mutton, horse meat, and boned fish. Visceral organs—heart, liver, and tripe—are good but if used in too large quantities may cause diarrhea (bones in large amounts have the same effect). Some veterinarians feel that pork is undesirable, while others consider lean pork acceptable as long as it is well cooked. Bacon drippings are often recommended for inclusion in the dog's diet, but this is a matter best discussed with your veterinarian since the salt in the bacon drippings might prove harmful to a dog that is not in good health. The "meat meal" used in some commercial foods is made from scrap meat processed at high temperatures and then dried. It is not quite so nutritious as fresh meat, but in combination with other protein products, it is an acceptable ingredient in the dog's diet.

Cooked eggs and raw egg yolk are good sources of protein, but raw egg white should never be fed since it may cause diarrhea. Cottage cheese and milk (fresh, dried, and canned) are high in protein, also. Puppies thrive on milk and it is usually included in the diet until the puppy is about three months of age, but when fed to older dogs it often causes diarrhea. Soy-bean meal, wheat germ meal, and dried brewers yeast are vegetable products high in protein and may be used to advantage in the dog's diet.

Vegetable and animal fats in moderate amounts should be used, especially if a main ingredient of the diet is dry or kibbled food. Fats should not be used excessively or the dog may become overweight. Generally, fats should be increased slightly in the winter and reduced somewhat during warm weather.

Carbohydrates are required for proper assimilation of fats. Dog biscuits, kibble, dog meal, and other dehydrated foods are good sources of carbohydrates, as are cereal products derived from rice, corn, wheat, and ground or rolled oats.

Vegetables supply additional proteins, vitamins, and minerals, and by providing bulk are of value in overcoming constipation. Raw or cooked carrots, celery, lettuce, beets, asparagus, tomatoes, and cooked spinach may be used. They should always be chopped or ground well and mixed with the other food. Various combinations may be used, but a good home-mixed ration for the mature dog consists of two parts of meat and one each of vegetables and dog meal (or cereal product).

Dicalcium phosphate and cod-liver oil are added to puppy diets to ensure inclusion of adequate amounts of calcium and Vitamins A and D. Indiscriminate use of dietary supplements is not only unjustified but may be harmful and many breeders feel that their over-use may lead to excessive growth as well as to overweight at maturity. Also, kidney damage in adult dogs has been traced to over-supplementation of the diet with calcium and Vitamin D.

Foods manufactured by well-known and reputable food processors are nutritionally sound and are offered in sufficient variety of flavors, textures, and consistencies that most dogs will find them tempting and satisfying. Canned foods are usually "ready to eat," while dehydrated foods in the form of kibble, meal, or biscuits may require the addition of water or milk. Dried foods containing fat sometimes become rancid, so to avoid an unpalatable change in flavor, the manufacturer may not include fat in dried food but recommend its addition at the time the water or milk is added.

Candy and other sweets are taboo, for the dog has no nutritional need for them and if he is permitted to eat them, he will usually eat less of foods he requires. Also taboo are fried foods, highly seasoned foods, and extremely starchy foods, for the dog's digestive tract is not equipped to handle them.

Frozen foods should be thawed completely and warmed at least to lukewarm, while hot foods should be cooled to lukewarm. Food should be in a fairly firm state, for sloppy food is difficult for the dog to digest.

Whether meat is raw or cooked makes little difference, so long as the dog is also given the juice that seeps from the meat during cooking. Bones provide little nourishment, although gnawing bones helps make the teeth strong and helps to keep tartar from accumulating on them. Beef bones, especially large knuckle bones, are best. Fish, poultry, and chop bones should never be given to dogs since they have a tendency to splinter and may puncture the dog's digestive tract.

Clean, fresh, cool water is essential and an adequate supply should be available twenty-four hours a day from the time the puppy is big enough to walk. Especially during hot weather, the drinking pan should be emptied and refilled at frequent intervals.

Puppies usually are weaned by the time they are six weeks old, so when you acquire a new puppy ten to twelve weeks old, he will already have been started on a feeding schedule. The breeder should supply exact details as to number of meals per day, types and amounts of food offered, etc. It is essential to adhere to this established routine, for drastic changes in diet may produce intestinal upsets. In most instances, a combination of dry meal, canned meat, and the plastic wrapped hamburger-like products provide a well-balanced diet. For a puppy that is too fat or too thin, or for one that has health problems, a veterinarian may recommend a specially formulated diet, but ordinarily, the commercially prepared foods can be used.

The amount of food offered at each meal must gradually be increased and by five months the puppy will require about twice what he needed at three months. However, the puppy should not be allowed to become too fat. Obesity has become a major health problem for dogs, and it is estimated that forty-one percent of American dogs are overweight. It is essential that weight be controlled throughout the dog's lifetime and that the dog be kept in trim condition—neither too fat nor too thin—for many physical problems can be traced directly to overweight. If the habit of overeating is developed in puppyhood, controlling the weight of the mature dog will be much more difficult.

A mature dog usually eats slightly less than he did as a growing puppy. For mature dogs, one large meal a day is usually sufficient, although some owners prefer to give two meals. As long as the dog enjoys optimum health and is neither too fat nor too thin, the number of meals a day makes little difference.

The amount of food required for mature dogs will vary. With canned dog food or home-prepared foods (that is, the combination of meat, vegetables, and meal), the approximate amount required is one-half ounce of food per pound of body weight. If the dog is fed a dehydrated commercial food, approximately one ounce of food is needed for each pound of body weight. Most manufacturers of commercial foods provide information on packages as to approximate daily needs of various breeds.

For most dogs, the amount of food provided should be increased slightly during the winter months and reduced somewhat during hot weather when the dog is less active.

As a dog becomes older and less active, he may become too fat. Or his appetite may decrease so he becomes too thin. It is necessary to adjust the diet in either case, for the dog will live longer and enjoy better health if he is maintained in trim condition. The simplest way to decrease or increase body weight is by decreasing or increasing the amount of fat in the diet. Protein content should be maintained at a high level throughout the dog's life.

If the older dog becomes reluctant to eat, it may be necessary to coax him with special food he normally relishes. Warming the food will increase its aroma and usually will help to entice the dog to eat. If he still refuses, rubbing some of the food on the dog's lips and gums may stimulate interest. It may be helpful also to offer food in smaller amounts and increase the number of meals per day. Foods that are highly nutritious and easily digested are especially desirable for older dogs. Small amounts of cooked, ground liver, cottage cheese, or mashed, hard-cooked eggs should be included in the diet often.

Before a bitch is bred, her owner should make sure that she is in optimum condition—slightly on the lean side rather than fat. The bitch in whelp is given much the same diet she was fed prior to breeding, with slight increases in amounts of meat, liver, and dairy products. Beginning about six weeks after breeding, she should be fed two meals per day rather than one, and the total daily intake increased. (Some bitches in whelp require as much as 50% more food than they consume normally.) She must not be permitted to become fat, for whelping problems are more likely to occur in overweight dogs. Cod-liver oil and dicalcium phosphate should be provided until after the puppies are weaned.

The dog used only occasionally for breeding will not require a special diet, but he should be well fed and maintained in optimum condition. A dog used frequently may require a slightly increased amount of food. But his basic diet will require no change so long as his general health is good and his flesh is firm and hard.

Dishes of this type are available in both plastic and stainless steel.

Crockery dish for food or water.

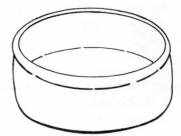

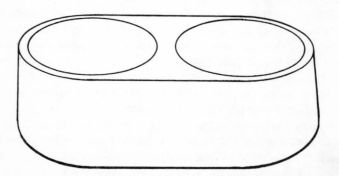

Stainless steel dish for food and water.

Maintaining the Dog's Health

In dealing with health problems, simple measures of preventive care are always preferable to cures—which may be complicated and costly. Many of the problems which afflict dogs can be avoided quite easily by instituting good dog-keeping practices in connection with feeding and housing.

Proper nutrition is essential in maintaining the dog's resistance to infectious diseases, in reducing susceptibility to organic diseases, and, of course, in preventing dietary deficiency diseases.

Cleanliness is essential in preventing the growth of disease-producing bacteria and other micro-organisms. All equipment, especially water and food dishes, must be kept immaculately clean. Cleanliness is also essential in controlling external parasites, which thrive in unsanitary surroundings.

Symptoms of Illness

Symptoms of illness may be so obvious there is no question that the dog is ill, or so subtle that the owner isn't sure whether there is a change from normal or not. **Loss of appetite, malaise** (general lack of interest in what is going on), **and vomiting** may be ignored if they occur singly and persist only for a day. However, in combination with other evidence of illness, such symptoms may be significant and the dog should be watched closely. **Abnormal bowel movements,** especially diarrhea or bloody stools, are causes for immediate concern. **Urinary abnormalities** may indicate infections, and bloody urine is always an indication of a serious condition. When a dog that has long been housebroken suddenly becomes incontinent, a veterinarian should be consulted, for he may be able to suggest treatment or medication that will be helpful.

Fever is a positive indication of illness and consistent deviation from the normal temperature range of 100 to 102 degrees is cause for concern. Have the dog in a standing position when taking his temperature. Coat the bulb of a rectal thermometer with petroleum jelly, raise the dog's tail, insert the thermometer to approximately half its length, and hold it in position for two minutes. Clean the thermometer with rubbing alcohol after each use and be sure to shake it down.

Fits, often considered a symptom of worms, may result from a variety of causes, including vitamin deficiencies, or playing to the point of exhaustion. A veterinarian should be consulted when a fit occurs, for it may be a symptom of serious illness.

Persistent coughing is often considered a symptom of worms, but may also indicate heart trouble—especially in older dogs.

Stary coat—dull and lackluster—indicates generally poor health and possible worm infestation. **Dull eyes** may result from similar conditions. Certain forms of blindness may also cause the eyes to lose the sparkle of vibrant good health.

Vomiting is another symptom often attributed to worm infestation. Dogs suffering from indigestion sometimes eat grass, apparently to induce vomiting and relieve discomfort.

Accidents and Injuries

Injuries of a serious nature—deep cuts, broken bones, severe burns, etc.—always require veterinary care. However, the dog may need first aid before being moved to a veterinary hospital.

A dog injured in any way should be approached cautiously, for reactions of a dog in pain are unpredictable and he may bite even a beloved master. A muzzle should always be applied before any attempt is made to move the dog or treat him in any way. The muzzle can be improvised from a strip of cloth, bandage, or even heavy cord, looped firmly around the dog's jaws and tied under the lower jaw. The ends should then be extended back of the neck and tied again so the loop around the jaws will stay in place.

A stretcher for moving a heavy dog can be improvised from a rug or board, and preferably two people should be available to transport it. A small dog can be carried by one person simply by grasping the loose skin at the nape of the neck with one hand and placing the other hand under the dog's hips.

Burns from chemicals should first be treated by flushing the coat with plain water, taking care to protect the dog's eyes and ears. A baking soda solution can then be applied to neutralize the chemical further. If the burned area is small, a bland ointment should be applied. If the burned area is large, more extensive treatment will be required, as well as veterinary care.

Burns from hot liquid or hot metals should be treated by applying a bland ointment, provided the burned area is small. Burns over large areas should be treated by a veterinarian.

Electric shock usually results because an owner negligently leaves an electric cord exposed where the dog can chew on it. If possible, disconnect the cord before touching the dog. Otherwise,

44

yank the cord from the dog's mouth so you will not receive a shock when you try to help him. If the dog is unconscious, artificial respiration and stimulants will be required, so a veterinarian should be consulted at once.

Fractures require immediate professional attention. A broken bone should be immobilized while the dog is transported to the veterinarian but no attempt should be made to splint it.

Poisoning is more often accidental than deliberate, but whichever the case, symptoms and treatment are the same. If the poisoning is not discovered immediately, the dog may be found unconscious. His mouth will be slimy, he will tremble, have difficulty breathing, and possibly go into convulsions. Veterinary treatment must be secured immediately.

If you find the dog eating something you know to be poisonous, induce vomiting immediately by repeatedly forcing the dog to swallow a mixture of equal parts of hydrogen peroxide and water. Delay of even a few minutes may result in death. When the contents of the stomach have been emptied, force the dog to swallow raw egg white, which will slow absorption of the poison. Then call the veterinarian. Provide him with information as to the type of poison, and follow his advice as to further treatment.

Some chemicals are toxic even though not swallowed, so before using a product, make sure it can be used safely around pets.

Severe bleeding from a leg can be controlled by applying a tourniquet between the wound and the body, but the tourniquet must be loosened at ten-minute intervals. Severe bleeding from head or body can be controlled by placing a cloth or gauze pad over the wound, then applying firm pressure with the hand.

To treat minor cuts, first trim the hair from around the wound, then wash the area with warm soapy water and apply a mild antiseptic such as tincture of metaphen.

Shock is usually the aftermath of severe injury and requires immediate veterinary attention. The dog appears dazed, lips and tongue are pale, and breathing is shallow. The dog should be wrapped in blankets and kept warm, and if possible, kept lying down with his head lower than his body.

Bacterial and Viral Diseases

Distemper takes many and varied forms, so it is sometimes difficult for even experienced veterinarians to diagnose. It is the number one killer of dogs, and although it is not unknown in older dogs, its victims are usually puppies. While some dogs do recover, permanent damage to the brain or nervous system is often sustained. Symptoms may include lethargy, diarrhea, vomiting, reduced appetite, cough, nasal discharge, inflammation of the eyes, and a rise in temperature. If distemper is suspected, a veterinarian must be consulted at once, for early treatment is essential. Effective preventive measures lie in inoculation. Shots for temporary immunity should be given all puppies within a few weeks after whelping, and the permanent inoculations should be given as soon thereafter as possible.

Hardpad has been fairly prevalent in Great Britain for a number of years, and its incidence in the United States is increasing. Symptoms are similar to those of distemper, but as the disease progresses, the pads of the feet harden and eventually peel. Chances of recovery are not favorable unless prompt veterinary care is secured.

Infectious hepatitis in dogs affects the liver, as does the human form, but apparently is not transmissible to man. Symptoms are similar to those of distemper, and the disease rapidly reaches the acute state. Since hepatitis is often fatal, prompt veterinary treatment is essential. Effective vaccines are available and should be provided all puppies. A combination distemper-hepatitis vaccine is sometimes used.

Leptospirosis is caused by a micro-organism often transmitted by contact with rats, or by ingestion of food contaminated by rats. The disease can be transmitted to man, so anyone caring for an afflicted dog must take steps to avoid infection. Symptoms include vomiting, loss of appetite, diarrhea, fever, depression and lethargy, redness of eyes and gums, and sometimes jaundice. Since permanent kidney damage may result, veterinary treatment should be secured immediately.

Rabies is a disease that is always fatal—and it is transmissible to man. It is caused by a virus that attacks the nervous system and is present in the saliva of an infected animal. When an infected animal bites another, the virus is transmitted to the new victim. It may also enter the body through cuts and scratches that come in contact with saliva containing the virus.

All warm-blooded animals are subject to rabies and it may be transmitted by foxes, skunks, squirrels, horses, and cattle as well as dogs. Anyone bitten by a dog (or other animal) should see his physician immediately, and health and law enforcement officials should be notified. Also, if your dog is bitten by another animal, consult your veterinarian immediately.

In most areas, rabies shots are required by law. Even if not required, all dogs should be given anti-rabies vaccine, for it is an effective preventive measure.

Dietary Deficiency Diseases

Rickets afflicts puppies not provided sufficient calcium and Vitamin D. Symptoms include lameness, arching of neck and back, and a tendency of the legs to bow. Treatment consists of providing adequate amounts of dicalcium phosphate and Vitamin D and exposing the dog to sunlight. If detected and treated before reaching an advanced stage, bone damage may be lessened somewhat, although it cannot be corrected completely.

Osteomalacia, similar to rickets, may occur in adult dogs. Treatment is the same as for rickets, but here, too, prevention is preferable to cure. Permanent deformities resulting from rickets or osteomalacia will not be inherited, so once victims recover, they can be used for breeding.

External Parasites

Fleas, lice, mites, and ticks can be eradicated in the dog's quarters by regular use of one of the insecticide sprays with a four to six weeks' residual effect. Bedding, blankets, and pillows should be laundered frequently and treated with an insecticide. Treatment for external parasites varies, depending upon the parasite involved, but a number of good dips and powders are available.

Fleas may be eliminated by dusting the coat thoroughly with flea powder at frequent intervals during the summer months when fleas are a problem.

Flea collars are very effective in keeping a dog free of fleas. However, some animals are allergic to the chemicals in the collars, so caution must be observed when the collar is used and the skin of the neck area must be checked frequently and the collar removed if the skin becomes irritated. Care must also be taken that the collar is not fastened too tightly, and any excess at the end must be cut off to prevent the dog from chewing it. The collar should be removed if it becomes wet (or even damp) and should always be removed before the dog is bathed and not replaced around the dog's neck again until the coat is completely dry. For a dog which reacts to the flea collar, a medallion to be hung from the regular collar is available. This will eliminate direct skin contact and thus any allergic reaction will be avoided. The medallion should, of course, be removed when the dog is bathed.

Lice may be eradicated by applying dips formulated especially for this purpose to the dog's coat. A fine-toothed comb should

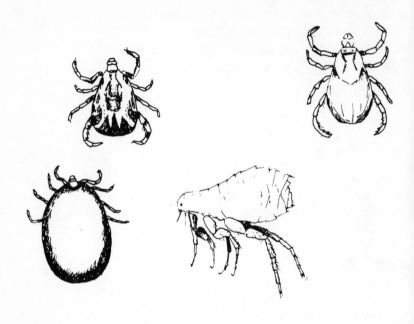

Common external parasites. Above, American dog ticks—left, female and right, male (much enlarged). Lower left, female tick, engorged. Lower right, dog flea (much enlarged).

then be used to remove dead lice and eggs, which are firmly attached to the coat.

Mites live deep in the ear canal, producing irritation to the lining of the ear and causing a brownish-black, dry type discharge. Plain mineral oil or ear ointment should be swabbed on the inner surface of the ear twice a week until mites are eliminated.

Ticks may carry Rocky Mountain spotted fever, so, to avoid possible infection, they should be removed from the dog only with tweezers and should be destroyed by burning (or by dropping them into insecticide). Heavy infestation can be controlled by sponging the coat daily with a solution containing a special tick dip.

Among other preparations available for controlling parasites on the dog's body are some that can be given internally. Since dosage must be carefully controlled, these preparations should not be used without consulting a veterinarian.

Internal Parasites

Internal parasites, with the exception of the tapeworm, may be transmitted from a mother dog to the puppies. Infestation may also result from contact with infected bedding or through access to a yard where an infected dog relieves himself. The types that may infest dogs are roundworms, whipworms, tapeworms, hookworms, and heartworms. All cause similar symptoms: a generally unthrifty appearance, stary coat, dull eyes, weakness and emaciation despite a ravenous appetite, coughing, vomiting, diarrhea, and sometimes bloody stools. Not all symptoms are present in every case, of course.

A heavy infestation with any type of worm is a serious matter and treatment must be started early and continued until the dog is free of the parasite or the dog's health will suffer seriously. Death may even result.

Promiscuous dosing for worms is dangerous and different types of worms require different treatment. So if you suspect your dog has worms, ask your veterinarian to make a microscopic examination of the feces, and to prescribe appropriate treatment if evidence of worm infestation is found.

LIFE CYCLE OF THE HEARTWORM

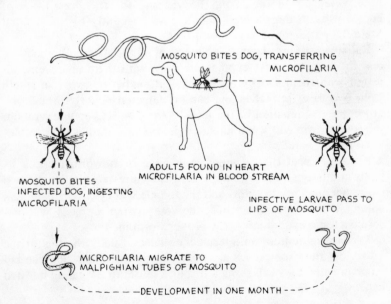

MATURE WORM   FILARIA AS FOUND IN BLOOD

MOSQUITO BITES DOG, TRANSFERRING MICROFILARIA

MOSQUITO BITES INFECTED DOG, INGESTING MICROFILARIA

ADULTS FOUND IN HEART
MICROFILARIA IN BLOOD STREAM

INFECTIVE LARVAE PASS TO LIPS OF MOSQUITO

MICROFILARIA MIGRATE TO MALPIGHIAN TUBES OF MOSQUITO

—DEVELOPMENT IN ONE MONTH—

Heartworms were once thought to be a problem confined to the Southern part of the United States but they have become an increasingly common problem in Middle Western States. The larva is transmitted from dog to dog through the bite of the mosquito, and eight to nine months may elapse from the time the dog is bitten until the heartworm is mature. Once they have entered the bloodstream, heartworms mature in the heart, where they interfere with heart action. Symptoms include lethargy, chronic coughing, and loss of weight. Having the dog's blood examined microscopically is the only way the tiny larvae (called microfilaria) can be detected. Eradication of heartworms is extremely difficult, so a veterinarian well versed in this field should be consulted. In an area where mosquitoes are prevalent, it is well to protect the dog by keeping him in a screened-in area.

Hookworms are found in puppies as well as adult dogs. When excreted in the feces, the mature worm looks like a thread and is about three-quarters of an inch in length. Eradication is a serious problem in areas where the soil is infested with the worms, for the dog may then become reinfested after treatment. Consequently, medication usually must be repeated at intervals, and the premises—including the grounds where the dog exercises—must be treated and must be kept well drained. You may wish to consult your veterinarian regarding the vaccine for the prevention of hookworms in dogs which was licensed recently by the United States Department of Agriculture.

Roundworms are the most common of all the worms that may infest the dog, for most puppies are born with them or become infested with them shortly after birth. Roundworms vary in length from two to eight inches and can be detected readily through microscopic examination of the feces. At maturity, upon excretion, the roundworm will spiral into a circle, but after it dies it resembles a cut rubber band.

If you suspect that a puppy may have roundworms, check its gums and tongue. If the puppy is heavily infested, the worms will cause anemia and the gums and the tongue will be a very pale pink color. If the puppy is anemic, the veterinarian probably will prescribe a tonic in addition to the proper worm medicine.

Tapeworms require an intermediate host, usually the flea or the louse, but they sometimes are found in raw fish, so a dog can become infested by swallowing a flea or a louse, or by eating infested fish.

LIFE CYCLE OF THE HOOKWORM

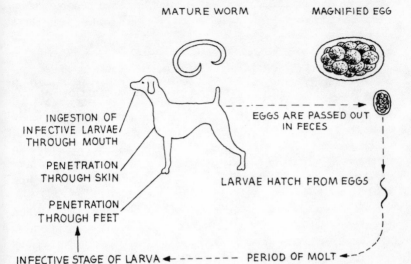

MATURE WORM

MAGNIFIED EGG

INGESTION OF
INFECTIVE LARVAE
THROUGH MOUTH

EGGS ARE PASSED OUT
IN FECES

PENETRATION
THROUGH SKIN

PENETRATION
THROUGH FEET

LARVAE HATCH FROM EGGS

INFECTIVE STAGE OF LARVA ← - - - - - - - PERIOD OF MOLT ← - -

LIFE CYCLE OF THE COMMON ROUNDWORM

MATURE WORM

EGG MAGNIFIED 400 TIMES

DOG INGESTS EMBRYONATED EGGS
SHELL DIGESTED OFF WORM IN DOGS STOMACH

EMBRYONATES IN 7 DAYS
IN WARM WEATHER

LARVA PENETRATES THROUGH
INTESTINE INTO BLOOD.
CIRCULATES FOR SEVERAL DAYS.

IS CAUGHT IN LUNGS, PENETRATES
THROUGH TO AIR SIDE OF LUNGS.

EMBRYO GROWS
TO MATURITY, LAYS
EGGS WHICH ARE PASSED
OUT IN FECES.

DOG COUGHS UP EMBRYO, SWALLOWS IT

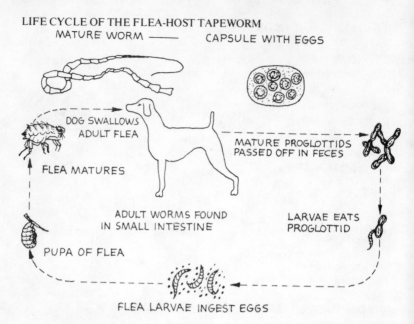

LIFE CYCLE OF THE FLEA-HOST TAPEWORM

MATURE WORM ———   CAPSULE WITH EGGS

DOG SWALLOWS ADULT FLEA

FLEA MATURES

MATURE PROGLOTTIDS PASSED OFF IN FECES

ADULT WORMS FOUND IN SMALL INTESTINE

LARVAE EATS PROGLOTTID

PUPA OF FLEA

FLEA LARVAE INGEST EGGS

A complete tapeworm can be two to three feet long. The head and neck of the tapeworm are small and threadlike, while the body is made up of segments like links of a sausage, which are about half an inch long and flat. Segments of the body separate from the worm and will be found in the feces or will hang from the coat around the anus and when dry will resemble dark grains of rice.

The head of the tapeworm is imbedded in the lining of the intestine where the worm feeds on the blood of the dog. The difficulty

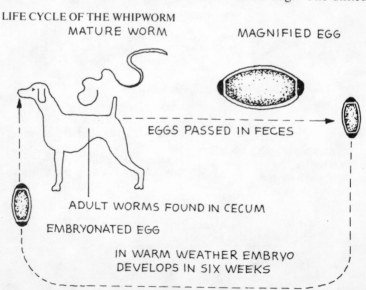

LIFE CYCLE OF THE WHIPWORM

MATURE WORM   MAGNIFIED EGG

EGGS PASSED IN FECES

ADULT WORMS FOUND IN CECUM

EMBRYONATED EGG

IN WARM WEATHER EMBRYO DEVELOPS IN SIX WEEKS

in eradicating the tapeworm lies in the fact that most medicines have a laxative action which is too severe and which pulls the body from the head so the body is eliminated with the feces, but the implanted head remains to start growing a new body. An effective medication is a tablet which does not dissolve until it reaches the intestine where it anesthetizes the worm to loosen the head before expulsion.

Whipworms are more common in the eastern states than in states along the West Coast, but whipworms may infest dogs in any section of the United States. Whipworms vary in length from two to four inches and are tapered in shape so they resemble a buggy whip—which accounts for the name.

At maturity, the whipworm migrates into the caecum, where it is difficult to reach with medication. A fecal examination will show whether whipworms are present, so after treatment, it is best to have several examinations made in order to be sure the dog is free of them.

Skin Problems

Skin problems usually cause persistent itching. However, **follicular mange** does not usually do so but is evidenced by moth-eaten-looking patches, especially about the head and along the back. **Sarcoptic mange** produces severe itching and is evidenced by patchy, crusty areas on body, legs, and abdomen. Any evidence suggesting either should be called to the attention of a veterinarian. Both require extensive treatment and both may be contracted by humans.

Allergies are not readily distinguished from other skin troubles except through laboratory tests. However, dog owners should be alert to the fact that various coat dressings and shampoos, or simply bathing the dog too often, may produce allergic skin reactions.

Eczema is characterized by extreme itching, redness of the skin and exudation of serous matter. It may result from a variety of causes, and the exact cause in a particular case may be difficult to determine. Relief may be secured by dusting the dog twice a week with a soothing powder containing a fungicide and an insecticide.

Other Health Problems

Clogged anal glands cause intense discomfort, which the dog may attempt to relieve by scooting himself along the floor on his haunches. These glands, located on either side of the anus, se-

crete a substance that enables the dog to expel the contents of the rectum. If they become clogged, they may give the dog an unpleasant odor and when neglected, serious infection may result. Contents of the glands can be easily expelled into a wad of cotton, which should be held under the tail with the left hand. Then, using the right hand, pressure should be exerted with the thumb on one side of the anus, the forefinger on the other. The normal secretion is brownish in color, with an unpleasant odor. The presence of blood or pus indicates infection and should be called to the attention of a veterinarian.

Eye problems of a minor nature—redness or occasional discharge—may be treated with a few drops of boric acid solution (2%) or salt solution (1 teaspoonful table salt to 1 pint sterile water). Cuts on the eyeball, bruises close to the eyes, or persistent discharge should be treated only by a veterinarian.

Heat exhaustion is a serious (and often fatal) problem caused by exposure to extreme heat. Usually it occurs when a thoughtless owner leaves the dog in a closed vehicle without proper shade and ventilation. Even on a day when outside temperatures do not seem excessively high, heat builds up rapidly to an extremely high temperature in a closed vehicle parked in direct sunlight or even in partial shade. Many dogs and young children die each year from being left in an inadequately ventilated vehicle. To prevent such a tragedy, an owner or parent should never leave a dog or child unattended in a vehicle even for a short time.

During hot weather, whenever a dog is taken for a ride in an air-conditioned automobile, the cool air should be reduced gradually when nearing the destination, for the sudden shock of going from cool air to extremely hot temperatures can also result in shock and heat exhaustion.

Symptoms of heat exhaustion include rapid and difficult breathing and near or complete collapse. After removing the victim from the vehicle, first aid treatment consists of sponging cool water over the body to reduce temperature as quickly as possible. Immediate medical treatment is essential in severe cases of heat exhaustion.

Care of the Ailing or Injured Dog

A dog that is seriously ill, requiring surgical treatment, transfusions, or intravenous feeding, must be hospitalized. One requiring less complicated treatment is better cared for at home, but it is essential that the dog be kept in a quiet environment. Preferably his bed should be in a room apart from family activity, yet close at hand, so his condition can be checked frequently. Clean bedding and adequate warmth are essential, as are a constant supply of fresh, cool water, and foods to tempt the appetite.

Special equipment is not ordinarily needed, but the following items will be useful in caring for a sick dog, as well as in giving first aid for injuries:

petroleum jelly	tincture of metaphen
rubbing alcohol	cotton, gauze, and adhesive tape
mineral oil	burn ointment
rectal thermometer	tweezers
hydrogen peroxide	boric acid solution (2%)

If special medication is prescribed, it may be administered in any one of several ways. A pill or small capsule may be concealed in a small piece of meat, which the dog will usually swallow with no problem. A large capsule may be given by holding the dog's mouth open, inserting the capsule as far as possible down the throat, then holding the mouth closed until the dog swallows. Liquid medicine should be measured into a small bottle or test tube. Then, if the corner of the dog's lip is pulled out while the head is tilted upward, the liquid can be poured between the lips and teeth, a small amount at a time. If he refuses to swallow, keeping the dog's head tilted and stroking his throat will usually induce swallowing.

Liquid medication may also be given by use of a hypodermic syringe without a needle. The syringe is slipped into the side of the mouth and over the rise at the back of the tongue, and the medicine is "injected" slowly down the throat. This is especially good for medicine with a bad taste, for the medicine does not touch the taste buds in the front part of the tongue. It also eliminates spills and guarantees that all the medicine goes in.

Foods offered the sick dog should be particularly nutritious and easily digested. Meals should be smaller than usual and offered at more frequent intervals. If the dog is reluctant to eat, offer food he particularly likes and warm it slightly to increase aroma and thus make it more tempting.

The Stone-Age Dog.

A Spotted Dog from India, ``Parent of the modern Coach Dog.''

History of the Genus Canis

The history of man's association with the dog is a fascinating one, extending into the past at least seventy centuries, and involving the entire history of civilized man from the early Stone Age to the present.

The dog, technically a member of the genus *Canis,* belongs to the zoological family group *Canidae,* which also includes such animals as wolves, foxes, jackals, and coyotes. In the past it was generally agreed that the dog resulted from the crossing of various members of the family *Canidae.* Recent findings have amended this theory somewhat, and most authorities now feel the jackal probably has no direct relationship with the dog. Some believe dogs are descended from wolves and foxes, with the wolf the main progenitor. As evidence, they cite the fact that the teeth of the wolf are identical in every detail with those of the dog, whereas the teeth of the jackal are totally different.

Still other authorities insist that the dog always has existed as a separate and distinct animal. This group admits that it is possible for a dog to mate with a fox, coyote, or wolf, but points out that the resulting puppies are unable to breed with each other, although they can breed with stock of the same genus as either parent. Therefore, they insist, it was impossible for a new and distinct genus to have developed from such crossings. They then cite the fact that any dog can be mated with any other dog and the progeny bred among themselves. These researchers point out, too, heritable characteristics that are different in these animals. For instance, the pupil of the eye of the fox is eliptical and vertical, while the pupil is round in the dog, wolf, and coyote. Tails, too, differ considerably, for tails of foxes, coyotes, and wolves always drop behind them, while those of dogs may be carried over the back or straight up.

Much conjecture centers on two wild dog species that still exist—the Dingo of Australia, and the Dhole in India. Similar in appearance, both are reddish in color, both have rather long, slender jaws, both have rounded ears that stand straight up, and both species hunt in packs. Evidence indicates that they had the same ancestors. Yet, today, they live in areas that are more than 4,000 miles apart.

Despite the fact that it is impossible to determine just when the dog first appeared as a distinct species, archeologists have found definite proof that the dog was the first animal domesticated by man. When man lived by tracking, trapping, and killing game, the dog added to the forces through which man discovered and captured the quarry. Man shared his primitive living quarters with the dog, and the two together devoured the prey. Thus, each helped to sustain the life of the other. The dog assisted man, too, by defending the campsite against marauders. As man gradually became civilized, the dog's usefulness was extended to guarding the other animals man domesticated, and, even before the wheel was invented, the dog served as a beast of burden. In fact, archeological findings show that aboriginal peoples of Switzerland and Ireland used the dog for such purposes long before they learned to till the soil.

Cave drawings from the palaeolithic era, which was the earliest part of the Old World Stone Age, include hunting scenes in which a rough, canine-like form is shown alongside huntsmen. One of these drawings is believed to be 50,000 years old, and gives credence to the theory that all dogs are descended from a primitive type ancestor that was neither fox nor wolf.

Archeological findings show that Europeans of the New Stone Age possessed a breed of dogs of wolf-like appearance, and a similar breed has been traced through the successive Bronze Age and Iron Age. Accurate details are not available, though, as to the external appearance of domesticated dogs prior to historic times (roughly four to five thousand years ago).

Early records in Chaldean and Egyptian tombs show that several distinct and well-established dog types had been developed by about 3700 B.C. Similar records show that the early people of the Nile Valley regarded the dog as a god, often burying it as a mummy in special cemeteries and mourning its death.

Some of the early Egyptian dogs had been given names, such as Akna, Tarn, and Abu, and slender dogs of the Greyhound type and a short-legged Terrier type are depicted in drawings found in Egyptian royal tombs that are at least 5,000 years old. The Afghan Hound and the Saluki are shown in drawings of only slightly later times. Another type of ancient Egyptian dog was much heavier and more powerful, with short coat and massive head. These

Bas-relief of Hunters with Nets and Mastiffs. From the walls of Assurbanipal's palace at Nineveh 668-626 B.C. *British Museum*.

probably hunted by scent, as did still another type of Egyptian dog that had a thick furry coat, a tail curled almost flat over the back, and erect "prick" ears.

Early Romans and Greeks mentioned their dogs often in literature, and both made distinctions between those that hunted by sight and those that hunted by scent. The Romans' canine classifications were similar to those we use now. In addition to dogs comparable to the Greek sight and scent hounds, the ancient Romans had Canes *villatici* (housedogs) and Canes *pastorales* (sheepdogs), corresponding to our present-day working dogs.

The dog is mentioned many times in the Old Testament. The first reference, in Genesis, leads some Biblical scholars to assert that man and dog have been companions from the time man was created. And later Biblical references bring an awareness of the diversity in breeds and types existing thousands of years ago.

As civilization advanced, man found new uses for dogs. Some required great size and strength. Others needed less of these characteristics but greater agility and better sight. Still others needed an accentuated sense of smell. As time went on, men kept those puppies that suited specific purposes especially well and bred them together. Through ensuing generations of selective breeding, desirable characteristics appeared with increasing frequency. Dogs used in a particular region for a special purpose gradually became more like each other, yet less like dogs of other areas used for different purposes. Thus were established the foundations for the various breeds we have today.

The American Kennel Club, the leading dog organization in the United States, divides the various breeds into six "Groups," based on similarity of purposes for which they were developed.

"Sporting Dogs" include the Pointers, Setters, Spaniels, and Retrievers that were developed by sportsmen interested in hunting game birds. Most of the Pointers and Setters are of comparatively recent origin. Their development parallels the development of sporting firearms, and most of them evolved in the British Isles. Exceptions are the Weimaraner, which was developed in Germany, and the Vizsla, or Hungarian Pointer, believed to have been developed by the Magyar hordes that swarmed over Central Europe a

Bas-relief of Assyrian Mastiffs hunting wild horses. *British Museum.*

thousand years ago. The Irish were among the first to use Spaniels, though the name indicates that the original stock may have come from Spain. Two Sporting breeds, the American Water Spaniel and the Chesapeake Bay Retriever, were developed entirely in the United States.

"Hounds," among which are Dachshunds, Beagles, Bassets, Harriers, and Foxhounds, are used singly, in pairs, or in packs to "course" (or run) and hunt for rabbits, foxes, and various rodents. But little larger, the Norwegian Elkhound is used in its native country to hunt big game—moose, bear, and deer.

The smaller Hound breeds hunt by scent, while the Irish Wolfhound, Borzoi, Scottish Deerhound, Saluki, and Greyhound hunt by sight. The Whippet, Saluki, and Greyhound are notably fleet of foot, and racing these breeds (particularly the Greyhound) is popular sport.

The Bloodhound is a member of the Hound Group that is known world-wide for its scenting ability. On the other hand, the Basenji is a comparatively rare Hound breed and has the distinction of being the only dog that cannot bark.

"Working Dogs" have the greatest utilitarian value of all modern dogs and contribute to man's welfare in diverse ways. The Boxer, Doberman Pinscher, Rottweiler, German Shepherd, Great Dane, and Giant Schnauzer are often trained to serve as sentries and aid police in patrolling streets. The German Shepherd is especially noted as a guide dog for the blind. The Collie, the various breeds of Sheepdogs, and the two Corgi breeds are known throughout the world for their extraordinary herding ability. And the exploits of the St. Bernard and Newfoundland are legendary, their records for saving lives unsurpassed.

The Siberian Husky, the Samoyed, and the Alaskan Malamute are noted for tremendous strength and stamina. Had it not been for these hardy Northern breeds, the great polar expeditions might never have taken place, for Admiral Byrd used these dogs to reach points inaccessible by other means. Even today, with our jet-age transportation, the Northern breeds provide a more practical means of travel in frigid areas than do modern machines.

"Terriers" derive their name from the Latin *terra,* meaning "earth," for all of the breeds in this Group are fond of burrowing. Terriers hunt by digging into the earth to rout rodents and fur-bearing animals such as badgers, woodchucks, and otters. Some breeds are expected merely to force the animals from their dens in

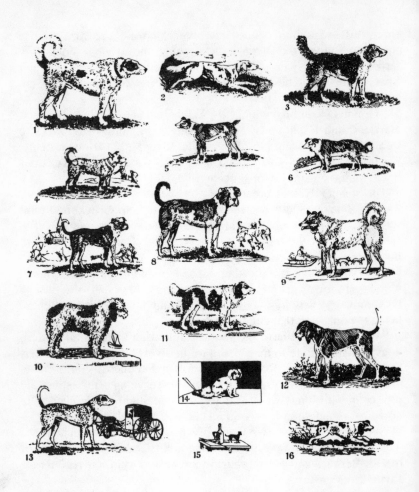

1. The Newfoundland. 2. The English Setter. 3. The Large Water-spaniel. 4. The Terrier. 5. The Cur-dog. 6. The Shepherd's Dog. 7. The Bulldog. 8. The Mastiff. 9. The Greenland Dog. 10. The Rough Water-dog. 11. The Small Water-spaniel. 12. The Old English Hound. 13. The Dalmatian or Coach-dog. 14. The Comporter (very much of a Papillon). 15. "Toy Dog, Bottle, Glass, and Pipe." *From a vignette.* 16. The Springer or Cocker. *From Thomas Bewick's "General History of Quadrupeds" (1790).*

order that the hunter can complete the capture. Others are expected to find and destroy the prey, either on the surface or under the ground.

Terriers come in a wide variety of sizes, ranging from such large breeds as the Airedale and Kerry Blue to such small ones as the Skye, the Dandie Dinmont, the West Highland White, and the Scottish Terrier. England, Ireland, and Scotland produced most of the Terrier breeds, although the Miniature Schnauzer was developed in Germany.

"Toys," as the term indicates, are small breeds. Although they make little claim to usefulness other than as ideal housepets, Toy dogs develop as much protective instinct as do larger breeds and serve effectively in warning of the approach of strangers.

Origins of the Toys are varied. The Pekingese was developed as the royal dog of China more than two thousand years before the birth of Christ. The Chihuahua, smallest of the Toys, originated in Mexico and is believed to be a descendant of the Techichi, a dog of great religious significance to the Aztecs, while the Italian Greyhound was popular in the days of ancient Pompeii.

"Non-Sporting Dogs" include a number of popular breeds of varying ancestry. The Standard and Miniature Poodles were developed in France for the purpose of retrieving game from water. The Bulldog originated in Great Britain and was bred for the purpose of "baiting" bulls. The Chow Chow apparently originated centuries ago in China, for it is pictured in a bas relief dated to the Han dynasty of about 150 B.C.

The Dalmatian served as a carriage dog in Dalmatia, protecting travelers in bandit-infested regions. The Keeshond, recognized as the national dog of Holland, is believed to have originated in the Arctic or possibly the Sub-Arctic. The Schipperke, sometimes erroneously described as a Dutch dog, originated in the Flemish provinces of Belgium. And the Lhasa Apso came from Tibet, where it is known as "Abso Seng Kye," the "Bark Lion Sentinel Dog."

During the thousands of years that man and dog have been closely associated, a strong affinity has been built up between the two. The dog has more than earned his way as a helper, and his faithful, selfless devotion to man is legendary. The ways in which the dog has proved his intelligence, his courage, and his dependability in situations of stress are amply recorded in the countless tales of canine heroism that highlight the pages of history, both past and present.

63

Dogs in Woodcuts. (*1st row*) (LEFT) "Maltese dog with shorter hair";
(RIGHT) "Spotted sporting dog trained to catch game"; (*2nd row*) (LEFT)
Sporting white dog; (RIGHT) "Spanish dog with floppy ears": (*3rd row*)
(LEFT) "French dog"; (RIGHT) "Mad dog of Grevinus"; (*4th row*) (LEFT)
Hairy Maltese dog; (RIGHT) "English fighting dog . . . of horrid aspect." *From
Aldrovandus (1637).*

History of the Bull Terrier

Few breeds have a more gory history than the lovable, affectionate, clownish Bull Terrier. In a way it seems amazing that a dog which was developed from strains used to torment and to kill other animals can today be such a grand pet and companion. Those qualities for which the ancestors of modern Bull Terriers were selected are the same qualities which when directed along less bloody avenues produce an unusually fine dog. Unfortunately, a large part of the general public is still prejudiced against the breed because of its heritage. It is worth reminding people that dogs of the past fought and killed because men wanted them to be fighters and killers. The history of the breed is an indictment of the human species, not of the Bull Terrier.

As the name clearly indicates, the Bull Terrier is a descendant of the Bulldog, but not of the type seen in the show ring today. The eighteenth and early nineteenth century Bulldog looked somewhat like a long-tailed Boxer. Descended from the old Mastiffs, these Bulldogs were built high on the leg and were great athletes. They had to be in order to survive, for their purpose in life was bull baiting. I am not going to discuss the details of a typical bull bait because they are too revolting. Several books have been written which give excellent descriptions of the various blood sports. Suffice it to say that until the Humane Act of 1835 put an end to them, bull baiting and the baiting of various other luckless creatures, notably bears and badgers, were popular forms of public entertainment in England. The worrying of the bull before it was slaughtered was supposed to improve the quality of the meat. Bulldogs were expected to attack the bull, which was chained or tied to restrict its movement, grab it by the nose, and pin the nose to the ground. Many of the dogs were tossed into the air and gored by the enraged bull. It took a courageous dog to continue the attack and to keep coming back for more punishment.

In the early nineteenth century, intentional crossbreeding of the Bulldog with various kinds of Terriers was done in order to pro-

Sir Wm. Verner's Tarquin, shown in New York in 1880. From *The Dog Book,* by Watson, 1906.

Old Dutch, Fred Hink's great sire, a pillar of the studbook. From *The Dog Book,* by Watson, 1906.

"Madman," Bull Terrier. From *The Dog,* by "Stonehenge," 1887.

Ch. Charney. From *The Dog Book,* by Watson, 1906.

duce a dog with greater agility and intelligence. These crosses resulted in a rather ugly but stout-hearted fellow known as the Bull and Terrier. When public baits of large animals were outlawed, interest increased in rat killing contests and in dog fighting, forms of "entertainment" which could easily be carried on clandestinely in a back room at the local pub. Dog "pits," where the fights took place, were constructed to definite specifications, and each fight was conducted according to very strict rules, for large sums of money were wagered on these fights and there was always danger of skulduggery. The Bull and Terrier, still possessing the terrible biting power of the Bulldog, but smaller, quick, and "game," was ideally suited for its new role. For these pit dogs, a process of selection operated in that only the most agile, tenacious, and quick-witted Bull and Terriers managed to survive long enough to reproduce and to pass down these virtues to their descendants. Gradually the dogs developed into a type similar in appearance to the modern Staffordshire Bull Terrier. It is important to note that Bull and Terriers came in all colors, including white.

In the 1850s, a James Hinks of Birmingham began experimenting with crosses between the Bull and Terrier and the White English Terrier. These White Terriers, now extinct, were intelligent and elegant, being very similar in conformation to the modern Manchester Terrier. The Dalmation and possibly other breeds were also used by Hinks in his experimental breedings. Eventually he produced an all-white strain which he named Bull Terriers. These dogs were far different from the original Bull and Terrier stock, having longer heads, smoother cheeks, straighter fronts, and much more overall "refinement." As might be expected, fanciers of the old Bull and Terrier didn't think much of Mr. Hinks' new breed. A challenge to a fight resulted in the now-famous battle of 1862 in which Hinks' "Puss" killed a dog of the old type while sustaining so few injuries herself that she was able to win several prizes at a dog show on the following day. "Puss's" victory indicated that the new white dogs had lost none of the fighting talent of their ancestors, and Hinks' Bull Terriers soon became very popular.

Pictures of Bull Terriers from the late 1800s reveal a dog very different from today's show specimen. The old-timers look high on the leg and less substantial. Heads, too, were much different. Most had a distinct stop and the eyes were larger and more rounded. Ears were invariably cropped, for the natural ear tended to be soft and either semi-erect or rose type. Then, in 1895, ear cropping was forbidden in England. Since the cropped ear gave the Bull Terrier a much smarter appearance, it was feared that the uncropped dogs would lose favor, which indeed they did. The dedicated fanciers, however, stuck by the breed and within five or six years succeeded in breeding some good dogs with naturally erect ears. Eventually the natural prick ear became so well established that the Standard was revised in 1930, making any ear type other than erect a fault.

A breed problem much more serious than ear carriage concerned ear function. As early as 1909, Bull Terrier breeders in England, disturbed at increasing numbers of deaf dogs, petitioned the Kennel Club to make deafness a disqualification at dog shows. Deafness in Bull Terriers and in other breeds where it occurs seems linked in some way with the white coat. Colored Bull Terriers are seldom, if ever, deaf. It was once thought that deafness could be eliminated from the breed by requiring breeders to pledge never to use a deaf dog for breeding and to destroy deaf puppies. But although breeders have conscientiously kept this pledge for over half a century, deaf puppies are still being born—not as often as in the early years but often enough to be a very real concern. Because the genes responsible for deafness seem to be recessive, a dog with normal hearing may be carrying the defect. Unfortunately, breeders are very reluctant to discuss abnormalities occurring in their litters, so the full extent of the problem is not really known. All breeders carefully test the hearing of White puppies before offering them for sale.

Modesty. From *The Dog Book,* by Watson, 1906.

While the White Bull Terrier continued to improve in type and increase in popularity, the old Bull and Terrier stock faded into the background but it did not disappear. The devotees of these brave, hardy dogs continued to breed them and in the 1930s the Bull and Terrier emerged with the status and "respectability" of a purebred, being given the name Staffordshire Bull Terrier. A much loved breed in England, the Staffordshire Bull Terrier is receiving increasing attention here in the United States, where it has recently been recognized by the AKC and taken into the Terrier Group. In addition to the major role which the Staffordshires played in the founding of the White Bull Terrier, they had a second vital part to play, and that was in the production of the Colored Bull Terrier. In the early 1900s, various Bull Terrier fanciers decided that it would be very desirable to have Colored dogs with the same conformation as the Whites. Whites were crossed to Staffordshires, thus regaining the brindle, red, fawn, and other colors. In going back to the old type for color, though, breeders also reintroduced many of the traits which Hinks and his successors had painstakingly bred out—pronounced stop; short, broad heads; round eyes; cheekiness; and various structural faults. The devotees of the Whites were, for the most part, violently opposed to the Coloreds for fear that interbreeding would cause loss of the pure white coat and general deterioration of the White stock. Although requested by the Bull Terrier Club to classify Coloreds as a separate breed, the Kennel Club in England refused, insisting that Coloreds and Whites be shown together as one breed. In England the first Colored champion was Lady Winifred, who earned her title in 1919. Gradually, by making use of the best Whites, the breeders of Colored Bull Terriers improved conformation and produced some great-headed dogs such as Romany Reliance in 1946. For breeders of Whites, however, there were strict sanctions against using Colored dogs or Whites with Colored ancestry in a White breeding program. Finally, in 1950, some of the more liberal and far-sighted breeders, who recognized that fear of "contamination" by the Coloreds was groundless and that inability to use the splendid Colored dogs or their White progeny was stifling breed progress, managed to have the restrictions voted out. Progress of the breed as a whole has been nothing less than phenomenal since that enlightened decision.

The Coloreds revitalized the Whites by restoring substance, pigmentation, and overall sturdiness. They also injected "the brindle factor" which had long been lost from the pure White strain. As stated in a previous chapter, almost all of the outstanding Bull Terriers of the past two decades have carried the brindle factor.

As early as the 1870s and 1880s, White Bull Terriers found their way here to the United States. They quickly attracted a loyal following and were recognized by the AKC in 1891. In 1897, the Bull Terrier Club of America was founded. With no ban on ear cropping here, Bull Terriers continued to be cropped until the 1930s. Pictures of several dogs with cropped ears appear in the Bull Terrier Club of America's *Annual* of 1939. American bred Bull Terriers tended to be more Terrier than Bull, longer legged, and lacking the down-faced, filled heads of their English contemporaries. Although English imports had always been important on the American scene, after World War II there arrived a series of British dogs who were of tremendous influence in improving heads, overall conformation, and quality. Today there are some truly excellent Bull Terriers being bred in America. These home breds, however, particularly our bitches, still lack, for the most part, the grand substance of the British Bull Terriers.

Here in the United States as in England, introduction of the Colored Bull Terrier was met with great hostility. Fearing corruption of the pure Whites, the Bull Terrier Club of America attempted to have the Coloreds classified as a different breed. In 1936 the AKC recognized the Colored Bull Terrier as a separate variety, and in 1937 Beltona Brindigal became the first Colored champion.

Even now, in the 1970s, there is dissension among breeders over the separate classification of the two varieties. Some breeders think that the Coloreds should not be considered a separate variety. For one thing, Coloreds usually produce White puppies as well as Colored puppies in their litters. Yet, under our present system, these litter mates cannot compete in the same ring. If Coloreds and Whites competed against each other, the Coloreds in particular but eventually also the Whites should improve in quality. Breeders of Whites often do not watch the judging of Coloreds and are most unlikely to ever consider using a Colored animal in a White breeding program. Yet the history of the breed shows that some of the finest Whites had a Colored parent! Ch. Beechhouse Snow Vision, Ch. Romany Romantic Vision, and Ch. Abraxas Audacity are but three examples.

There are many other breeders, however, who strongly oppose combining the two varieties. Certainly it would be much more difficult to make a Colored champion if a Colored had to defeat Whites, since at the present time the overall quality of the Whites is considerably higher than that of the Coloreds. Nor do some breeders of Coloreds or of Whites want to lose representation in the Terrier Group where both varieties are now able to compete.

Perhaps in the near future there will be a meeting of minds and breeders will agree that the only important thing is improvement of the breed through the breeding of better Bull Terriers, regardless of their color.

Ch. Monkery's Mr. Frosty of Ormandy.

Ch. Souperlative Laura.

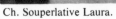
Ch. Monkery's Caspian, sire of Moonride and Minx.

Bull Terriers in England

The Bull Terrier is native to England, having originated there in the 1850s under the inspiration and breeding skill of James Hinks. Over a period of a hundred years, the Bull Terrier gradually evolved into the splendid creature he is today. A few dozen talented, dedicated breeders were responsible for his metamorphosis from an animal resembling Hinks' "Madman" to animals such as Romany Robin Goodfellow, Ormandy Souperlative Bar Sinister, and their present-day descendants. There are several excellent books devoted entirely to the history of the breed in England. They are all well worth reading.

There is still tremendous enthusiasm for Bull Terriers in England. The Bull Terrier Club boasts a world-wide membership of over fifteen hundred fanciers. In the homes and kennels of British breeders live the most magnificent Bull Terriers in the world. Anyone who doubts this need only visit and see for himself the four-legged residents at Abraxas, Agates, Hollyfir, Maerdy, Monkery, Ormandy, Romany, Souperlative, and other great kennels. It is only within the past eight or nine years that American home breds have had a ghost of a chance of defeating English imports at our AKC shows.

There are undoubtedly many reasons for the superiority of British Bull Terriers. Foremost has been the availability of the very best breeding stock—particularly, good bitches well suited to the excellent dogs. In addition, the English breeders have the skill to mate "the best to the best" and to come up consistently with an improved product. Perhaps yet another reason is that the successful breeders establish breeding programs with a purpose and work toward achieving definite goals. And finally, it seems to me that the stimulus of really keen competition has been at work, operating as it does to inspire toward the achievement of excellence.

The Regent Trophy is probably the most coveted award that a Bull Terrier can win. Dr. Geoffrey Vevers donated the trophy in 1930 to recognize the best Bull Terrier first shown during the previous year. (In January 1977 the trophy was awarded to a dog first shown during 1976.) In giving this trophy, Dr. Vevers accomplished two important things: first, he provided a handsome

Ch. Targyt Silver
Bob of Langville,
1968 Regent Trophy
winner, now owned
by Kenneth Neu-
man.

trophy, and a coveted honor to which all serious breeders could aspire; second, he assured the continued production of worthy young stock since the same dogs cannot compete twice.

In 1947, Mr. Raymond Oppenheimer gave the Ormandy Jugs for the best dog and bitch exhibited at a championship show the previous year, but not necessarily exhibited for the first time. This provided the opportunity for a slowly maturing Bull Terrier which might be too immature to win the Regent Trophy to compete for and possibly win the Ormandy Jug the following year. Bull Terriers competing for the major trophies do so by invitation of The Bull Terrier Club. Winners of the Regent Trophy and the Ormandy Jugs in recent years are as follows:

1965

Regent Trophy: Ch. Ormandy's Barbelle by Bar Sinister ex Ch. Burson's Belinda by Ormandy's Souperlative Princeling. Breeders—W. G. and P. Burford.

Dog Jug: Meltdown Moonshiner by Bar Sinister ex Meltdown Princely Gift by Ormandy's Souperlative Princeling. Breeder—Mrs. Treen.

Bitch Jug: Ch. Ormandy's Barbelle.

1966

Regent Trophy: Souperlative Rominten Rhinegold by Ch. Ormandy's Ben of Highthorpe ex Ch. Souperlative Sprig by Souperlative Acetylene. Breeder—Mrs. Chisnall.

Dog Jug: Ch. Monkery's Mr. Frosty of Ormandy by Bar Sinister ex Ch. Monkery's Snowflake of Ormandy by Ch. Ormandy's Ben of Highthorpe. Breeder—Mrs. P. Holmes.

Bitch Jug: Souperlative Rominten Rhinegold.

1967

Regent Trophy: White Knight of Lenster by Bar Sinister ex Rombus Allegro by Souperlative Brinhead. Breeder—Miss D. Caunce.

Ch. Abraxas Audacity, 1970 Regent Trophy winner, shown winning "Supreme Champion"—Best in Show at Crufts, 1971.

Dog Jug: Denspur's Sheikh by Souperlative Acetylene ex Denspur's Slyph by Denspur's Heir Presumptive. Breeder—R. Spurden.

Bitch Jug: Ch. Contango Clever Me by Bar Sinister ex Ch. Contango Quelle Chance by Ch. Romany Romantic Vision. Breeder—Mrs. A. W. Schuster.

1968

Regent Trophy: Ch. Targyt Silver Bob of Langville by Langville Pilot Officer ex Estelle of Langville by Ch. Souperlative Sea Captain. Breeder—G. S. Gratty.

Dog Jug: Ch. Targyt Silver Bob of Langville.

Bitch Jug: Uglee Apple Blossom by Ch. Ormandy's Ben of Highthorpe ex Souperlative Cyclamen by Ch. Abraxas Anthus. Breeder—Mrs. Chamberlain.

1969

Regent Trophy: Ch. Tejaycey Blanco Santa by Ch. Ormandy's Archangel ex Ch. Ormandy's Corinthian Clipper by Ch. Ormandy's Ben of Highthorpe. Breeder—T. J. Cochrane.

Dog Jug: Ch. Bank Top Julius by Ch. Romany River Pirate ex Denspur's Salome by Ch. Monkery's Mr. Frosty of Ormandy. Breeder—E. Judd.

Bitch Jug: Ch. Tejaycey Blanco Santa.

1970

Regent Trophy: Ch. Abraxas Audacity by Ch. Romany River Pirate ex Ch. Abraxas Athenia by Ch. Monkery's Mr. Frosty of Ormandy. Breeder—Miss V. Drummond-Dick.

Dog Jug: Ch. Abraxas Audacity.

Bitch Jug: Ch. Iella Cinderella by Ch. Monkery's Mr. Frosty of Ormandy ex Valkyrie Zenith by Ormandy's Caunsul Cavalier. Breeder—E. H. Hughes.

Ch. Abraxas Aristo,
1971 Regent Trophy
winner.

1971

Regent Trophy: Ch. Abraxas Aristo by Woodrow Frosty Flake of Ormandy ex Ch. Abraxas Athenia by Ch. Monkery's Mr. Frosty of Ormandy. Breeder—Miss V. Drummond-Dick.

Dog Jug: Maerdy Mycropolis by Souperlative Benbeau of Ormandy ex Maerdy Mona by Ormandy's Souperlative Bar Sinister. Breeder—W. Morgan.

Bitch Jug: Ch. Souperlative Laura by Ch. Romany River Pirate ex Ch. Souperlative Rominten Rhinegold by Ch. Ormandy's Ben of Highthorpe. Breeder—Miss E. M. Weatherill.

1972

Regent Trophy: Ch. Abraxas Achilles by Ch. Ormandy's Archangel ex Ch. Abraxas Athenia by Ch. Monkery's Mr. Frosty of Ormandy. Breeder—Miss V. Drummond-Dick.

Dog Jug: Ch. Abraxas Achilles.

Bitch Jug: Ch. Agates Sweet Sauce by Ch. Ormandy's Caviar ex Ch. Agates Amethyst by Ch. Ormandy's Thunderflash. Breeder—Mrs. M. O. Sweeten.

1973

Regent Trophy: Monkery's Delantero Moon Ride by Ch. Monkery's Caspian ex Delantero Lunar Princess by Ch. Meltdown Moonshiner. Breeder—Mrs. M. B. Howard-Williams.

Dog Jug: Monkery's Delantero Moon Ride.

Bitch Jug: Ch. Woodrow Minx by Ch. Monkery's Caspian ex Souperlative Wren of Woodrow by Ch. Monkery's Mr. Frosty of Ormandy. Breeder—Miss H. Powell.

Eng. and Am. Ch. Abraxas Achilles,
1972 Regent Trophy winner, owned by
Ralph and Mary Bowles.

Monkery's Delantero Moon Ride, 1973 Regent Trophy winner.

Ch. Badlesmere Bonaparte of Ormandy, 1974 Regent Trophy winner.

1974

Regent Trophy: Ch. Badlesmere Bonaparte of Souperlative by Ch. Maerdy Maestro ex Souperlative Booksale Angel's Tears by Ch. Abraxas Audacity. Breeder—Mrs. J. Shaw. Owners—Mr. R. H. Oppenheimer and Miss E. Weatherill.

Dog Jug: Ch. Badlesmere Bonaparte of Souperlative.

Bitch Jug: Ch. Brobar Elite by Ch. Maerdy Maestro ex Brobar Horatia by Ch. Brobar Headliner. Breeder—J. A. Miller. Owners—Mr. and Mrs. Porter.

1975

Regent Trophy: Ch. Curraneye Schoolgirl by Ch. Souperlative Sunstar of Ormandy ex Curraneye Lively Lady by Ch. Curraneye Independence. Breeder-Owner—Mrs. E. Micklethwaite.

Dog Jug: Ch. Hollyfir's Devil's Disciple by Ch. Maerdy Maestro of Ormandy ex Ch. Sweet Thursday of Hollyfir by Langville Pilot Officer. Breeders—Mr. and Mrs. J. Mildenhall. Owner—R. Hill.

Bitch Jug: Ch. Keyhole Kate of Brobar by Recnad Silver Oak ex Pollyanna of Brobar by Ch. Maerdy Maestro of Ormandy. Breeder—Mrs. Fielding. Owners—Mr. and Mrs. A. Miller.

1976

Regent Trophy: Ch. Jobrulu Jacobinia by Ch. Badlesmere Bonaparte of Souperlative ex Jobrulu Xotica by Ch. Souperlative Sunstar of Ormandy. Breeder-Owner: Mrs. J. Kenway.

Dog Jug: Ch. Jobrulu Jacqueminot (litter brother to Regent Trophy winner).

Bitch Jug: Souperlative Evanly of Sax by Ch. Maerdy Maestro of Ormandy ex Ch. Souperlative Scrumptious of Ormandy by Ch. Ionem Corvette. Breeder—Miss E. M. Weatherill. Owner—Mr. T. Degg.

Ch. Agates Sweet Sauce.

Other major trophies not listed here because of space limitations are the Coverwood Casket for Runner-Up in the Regent Trophy, The Golden State Trophy for Best of Opposite Sex in the Regent Trophy, the Charlie Girl Cup for Best Mover in the major trophies, and the Sandawana Trophy for the Best Colored Bull Terrier each year.

Most of today's leading kennels are represented in the list of trophy winners from 1965 to date, if not as breeders of the winners then as having bred the sire or dam or grandsire of the winners. Let's briefly identify some of these outstanding kennels and their best known dogs.

Abraxas: Miss Violet Drummond-Dick has enjoyed the singular accomplishment of having bred three successive Regent Trophy winners, all from the same dam, the beautiful Ch. Abraxas Athenia. The 1970 winner, Ch. Abraxas Audacity, also made history by going Best in Show at Crufts, the largest dog show in the world, the first Bull Terrier to be so recognized. Abraxas has also produced lovely bitches such as Aurora, Amoret, and Ch. Abraxas Arietta. Exported to the United States have been the important stud dogs U. S. Ch. Abraxas Ace of Aces, English and U. S. Ch. Abraxas Achilles, U. S. Ch. Abraxas Antonius, and others yet to be shown.

Agates: Mrs. Margaret Sweeten usually has a dog competing for the major trophies. Ch. Agates Amethyst, a daughter of Thunderflash, is one of her best efforts, having produced, when mated

Langville Pilot Officer.

Ch. Woodrow Minx.

to Ch. Ormandy's Caviar, the beautiful brother and sister Ch. Agates Bismarck and Ch. Agates Sweet Sauce. Exported to the United States, Agates Bronzino obtained his championship in eleven days and had an unusually successful show career. Agates Silver Tassie is the most recent Agates import.

Brobar: Mr. and Mrs. J. A. Miller are the breeders of the 1974 Bitch Jug winner, Ch. Brobar Elite. Other well known Brobar dogs are Ch. Keg of Brobar, Ch. Brobar Booster, Ch. Brobar Buccaneer, Ch. Brobar Warpaint, and Ch. Brobar Headliner, grandsire of Elite.

Crossmatch: Mr. G. Taylor is the breeder of Ch. Crossmatch Craftsman, Ch. Crossmatch Magic Coat of Lenster (sire of two brindles now in the United States), and Crossmatch Colour Me Gay.

Delantero: Mrs. Howard-Williams sent her Delantero Lunar Princess to Ch. Monkery's Caspian and in the resulting litter was the 1973 Regent Trophy and Dog Jug winner Ch. Monkery's Delantero Moonride!

Denspur: Mr. R. Spurden is the breeder of the 1967 Dog Jug winner Ch. Denspur's Sheikh. He also bred Denspur's Summer Sky, the dam of Ch. Bank Top Julius.

Hollyfir: Betty and Jack Mildenhall are breeders of Sweet Thursday of Hollyfir, Ch. Hollyfir's Dog in a Doublet, Hollyfir's Witch's Cub (now in Canada), Ch. Hollyfir Devil's Disciple, Ch. Hollyfir Mephisto, and Hollyfir Devil's General.

Iella: Mr. E. S. T. Hughes bred the Bitch Jug winner of 1970, Iella Cinderella. Her litter sister, Iella Desdamona, sent to Canada, is the dam of the excellent litter which contained Ch. Sunburst Solar System, the 1972 Silverwood winner.

Jobrulu: Mrs. J. Kenway bred her lovely bitch Jobrulu's Xotica to Bonaparte to produce both the Regent Trophy and Dog Jug winners of 1976—Ch. Jobrulu Jacobinia and Ch. Jobrulu Jacqueminot.

Kashdowd: Mrs. I. Higgs bred Ch. Kashdowd Double Star of Waterston. Her prefix is best known to Americans, however, through the two imports Ch. Kashdowd Bounce and Canadian Ch. Kashdowd Valkyrie Velvet.

Kearby: Mrs. Youatt's Ch. Kearby Gabriel, Ch. Kearby's Magnum, Ch. Kearby's Jeremy, and Ch. Kearby's Temptress are well known in England, but the Kearby prefix is not found in many pedigrees of American dogs.

Lenster-Phidgity-Harpers: The combined talents of Mrs. Mankin, recently deceased, Mrs. Graham-Weall, and Miss Dot Vick have produced a great many Bull Terriers of great impact on the breed both in England and in the United States. Anyone studying the history of the breed will find these three kennel names appearing many times in the pedigrees of most of the best dogs both in England and in the United States. Although it is not possible to list all of the famous dogs bred or owned by this kennel, a partial list is enough to indicate its importance. Check your own dog's pedigree and you will probably find one or more of the following: Ch. Phidgity Phlasher of Lenster, Ch. Gazur Phidgity Constellation, Ch. Phidgity Snow Dream, Ch. Phidgity Flashlight of Wentwood, Ch. Phidgity Shepherd Boy, Ch. Harper's Hat Trick of Lenster, White Knight of Lenster, Ch. Crossmatch Magic Coat of

Ch. Romany River Pirate.

Ch. Romany River Music.

Lenster, Ch. Rombus Astronaut of Lenster, Harper's Howda of Lenster, and American and Canadian Ch. Harper's Hemstitch!

Maerdy: Bill Morgan is breeding some of today's outstanding Bull Terriers such as Ch. Maerdy Melba, Ch. Maerdy Mystic Maid, Maerdy Mona, Ch. Maerdy Mycropolis, and Ch. Maerdy Maestro, sire of both the dog and bitch in the 1974 major trophies. Maerdy has sent at least two excellent Bull Terriers to Canada—Ch. Maerdy Moonstone and Ch. Maerdy Magdalene. In California is Maerdy Montrose, a great headed dog.

Meltdown: Mrs. M. Treen's important contributions to the breed include Meltdown Cerisette, Ch. Meltdown Moonshiner, Ch. Meltdown Conwood Cherry Ripe, Meltdown Beauty Spot, and Meltdown Princely Gift, and English and American Ch. Monkery Meltdown Sea Shanty.

Monkery: Mrs. P. E. Holmes is well known for the dogs Monkery North Sea, Ch. Monkery's Caspian, Ch. Monkery's Delantero Moon Ride, and Monkery's Endora. But when she bred Ch. Monkery's Snowflake of Ormandy to Bar Sinister and thereby produced Ch. Monkery Mr. Frosty of Ormandy, she gave the breed a dog who was to become a stud force of the greatest importance. He produced such beautiful daughters as Ch. Abraxas Athenia, Ch. Maerdy Mystic Maid, Ch. Iella Cinderella, Ormandy's Snowdrop, Uglee Snow Blossom, and others who are not so famous but who have produced outstanding offspring. His most illustrious sons were Woodrow Frosty Flake of Ormandy, Iella Rockafella, Booksale Colonial Boy, and Ch. Souperlative Concorde of Ormandy. Important Monkery dogs now in the United States are Ch. Monkery Sea Link and his two sons Ch. Monkery Sea Boots and English Ch. Monkery Meltdown Sea Shanty.

Ormandy, Souperlative: Mr. Raymond Oppenheimer and Miss Eva Weatherill are without doubt the two best known Bull Terrier breeders in the world. Since Ormandy won its first challenge certificate in 1937, Mr. Oppenheimer's success as a breeder has been phenomenal. He began by buying the best possible bitches—a lesson to anyone seriously interested in breeding. A history of the evolution of Bull Terriers from the time he entered the breed will be found in Mr. Oppenheimer's informative and entertaining book *McGuffin and Co.* This and its sequel, *After Bar Sinister,* should be on the bookshelf of every Bull Terrier fancier. During World War II, Eva Weatherill joined forces with Ormandy and began breeding under her own prefix, Souperlative. Many of the key Bull Terriers bear both names. Just a few of these key dogs bred or owned by Ormandy-Souperlative are: Ch. Ormandy Souperlative Snowflash, Ormandy Souperlative Bar Sinister (possibly the best Bull Terrier ever), Ch. Souperlative Brinhead, Ch. Ormandy Souperlative Princeling, Ch. Souperlative Summer Queen, Ch. Souperlative Sunshine, Ch. Souperlative Rominten Rhinegold, Ch. Souperlative Scrumptious of Ormandy, Ch. Monkery's Mr. Frosty of Ormandy, Ch. Maerdy Maestro of Ormandy, and the list could go on and on!

Romany: Miss D. Montague Johnstone and Miss Margaret Williams are a team unequalled in the history of Bull Terrier breeding, particularly the breeding of Colored Bull Terriers. Romany dogs have made tremendous contributions to the breed in the past

Ormandy Souperlative Bar Sinister.

Ch. Abraxas Athenia, dam of three Regent Trophy winners—Audacity, Aristo, and Achilles.

and continue to be a vital force at the present. Since the 1940s Romany has been the undisputed leader in the breeding of Coloreds. Some of the best known Romany dogs are Rhinestone, Reliance, Rather Lovely, Rather Likely, Refreshed, Refresher, Rhinegold, and Robinsonya. Robinsonya's son, Ch. Romany Robin Goodfellow, is behind almost all of today's leading dogs through his two White sons born to two litter sisters. Bred to Ch. Phidgity Snow Dream he produced Ch. Romany Romantic Vision, who is behind just about every leading dog today in both England and the United States. Bred to Ch. Phidgity Flashlight of Wentwood he produced U. S. Ch. Krackton Robin of Wentwood, sire of twenty U.S. champions during the 1960s and behind many American dogs today. Romany's current leading stud dog, Ch. Romany River Pirate, has sired Ch. Bank Top Julius, Ch. Abraxas Audacity, Ch. Hollyfir's Dog in a Doublet, Ch. Souperlative Laura, Romany River Music (also proving an excellent sire), and other important dogs including Canadian Ch. Maerdy Moonstone, and in the United States, Ch. Arundela Cardinal and Harpers Hawkeye of Phidgity.

Perhaps this all too brief review of the leading English kennels and their great dogs has provided some understanding of how essential English Bull Terriers have been and still are to the progress of the breed here in the United States.

Ch. Killer Joe, bred and owned by Peggy and Michael Arnaud.

Int. Ch. Comanche of Upend with owner, Susan Meller.

Banbury Bachelor's Button, by Souperlative Silver Spoon ex Banbury Blossom.

Bull Terriers on Other Continents

Apart from the British Isles, where we have seen that the Bull Terrier is indeed one of the leading breeds, other European countries are becoming increasingly interested in our unique Terriers. At the close of World War II, there were very few Bull Terriers remaining on the Continent, and therefore, most of the dogs in Europe today are imports from England or descendants of those imports.

In Austria, Germany, Belgium, Holland, and Italy there are enthusiastic breeders and exhibitors. In Germany, for example, the Bull Terrier Club had over three hundred members in 1970. This was about the same as the membership in the Bull Terrier Club of America! It is interesting to note that Colored Bull Terriers are preferred, particularly in Germany. The Colored bitch Kearby's Amazon is behind about one-third of the German Bull Terriers. Dr. Dieter Fleig of Alemannentrutz Kennels in Platiss, West Germany, is one of the breed's staunchest supporters. He has studied the breed in his country and come up with the interesting statistic that about seventy-five percent of the Bull Terriers in Germany are Coloreds. Farm Kennels in Belgium and in The Netherlands have an excellent foundation bitch in Judyandrea of Lenster. In Belgium, in The Netherlands, and in Germany, the championship shows often have very good entries of Bull Terriers.

In Italy the leading kennel appears to be Matedy owned by Dr. Mayer-Chellini of Spinetta Marengo. He owns some very good Bull Terriers, such as International Champions Romany Rising Tumult, Romany Romantic Troubadour, Souperlative Comus Curara, Dahrel Sweet Sherry, and Ormandy's Krackton Kamelot.

It is only natural to expect that wherever there is a large British population there should also be good representation of Bull Terriers. So it is not surprising to learn that the breed is held in high esteem in South Africa, Australia, and New Zealand.

In Rhodesia the leading kennel is Sandawana, owned by Mr. Dave Harrison and Mr. W. Baron. Among the leading dogs in Rhodesia are Champions Sandawana's Cobber, Sandawana's

Ch. Kashdowd Bounce, owned by W. E. Mackay-Smith.

Avion Perry, and Sandawana's Tamzin. Their stock is closely related to the English dogs through several imports including Ch. Keg of Brobar. Apparently the Bull Terrier is very well suited to the climate in southern Africa, just another one of the many qualities making him a favorite there.

The Bull Terrier situation in Australia is probably similar to what it was in the United States twenty or even ten years ago. Fanciers have imported many dogs from England, but they have been mostly males so that the breed has been lacking in good brood bitches. Also, since Australia is larger in area than the United States, there is a problem of distance separating breeders. Mr. Tom Horner, a well known English judge and former breeder of Tartary Bull Terriers, judged the breed in Australia in 1974 and was pleased

Ch. Belle Terre's Patience, owned by H. Wm. Schmitz.

Ch. Canterbury's Mack The Knife, owned by Trudi Tamburri.

Mack's daughter, Aliquippa Queen of Mingo, owned by Alma Mason.

with some excellent dogs he saw, notably Dabews Thundercloud, a grandson of Romany River Music. Thundercloud was bred by Mr. Beioley of Melbourne, Victoria. Other Bull Terrier kennels in Australia are Budrun, Gilavon, Xipheres, Kramlla, Noseelg, Jockrobbie, Andaedo, Bomont, and Mialyn.

The Bull Terrier Club of New Zealand was formed in 1971. However, I have no other information about their Bull Terrier activities.

Venezuela may have the largest numbers of Bull Terriers in South America. A well known American "all rounder" judge mentioned judging about thirty dogs at a show there in 1974. This judge, who knows our breed very well, said that some of the Bull Terriers were of excellent quality.

Ch. Magor The Marquis, Best American Bred Bull Terrier at the 1976 Silverwood Competition.   Breeders-owners, Gordon and Norma Smith.

Holcroft Kowhai Lottie on her twelfth birthday.   Dam of Ch. Killer Joe and four other champions.

The Silverwood Trophy Competition

In September 1970, the first Major Trophy Show was held in the United States. This show was designed to be comparable to the Regent Trophy Show held in England each year. The impetus for such a show in this country really came from the British breeders, and it was the Bull Terrier Club in England which offered the first two major trophies—the Silverwood Trophy and the Raydium Brigadier Trophy.

The Silverwood Trophy is a handsome carved wooden White Bull Terrier mounted on a base where the names of the winners are inscribed. The trophy is awarded each year to the best American Bred Bull Terrier—that is, a Bull Terrier whelped on the North American Continent. Canadian and United States dogs compete. The name "Silverwood" was chosen in honor of Mr. and Mrs. William Colket, who owned the Silverwood Kennels in West Chester, Pennsylvania. A former President of the Bull Terrier Club of America, respected breeder-judge, and Bull Terrier columnist for *Purebred Dogs*, Mr. Colket was active in the breed for many years. While on a judging assignment in England, Mr. Colket had discussed with Mr. Raymond Oppenheimer the possibility of having a major trophy show in the United States. But before any concrete plans were developed, both Mr. and Mrs. Colket were killed in automobile accidents within a few months of each other during 1969. Shortly thereafter, the Bull Terrier Club in England offered the two trophies to the Bull Terrier Club of America in memory of the Colkets. Since Mr. Oppenheimer was scheduled to judge the BTCA Specialty Show at Ox Ridge in Darien, Connecticut, in the fall of 1970, it was decided to hold the first Trophy Show on the same weekend. In that way Mr. Oppenheimer would be on hand to make the presentation of the trophies on behalf of the English club.

The Raydium Brigadier Trophy is given for Best of Opposite Sex to the Best American Bred Bull Terrier. This trophy is to honor the memory of Mrs. Gladys Adlam (Brendon Bull Terriers) and Mrs. Jessie Bennett (Coolyn Hill Bull Terriers). This trophy is also a Bull Terrier figurine, a replica of the first Regent Trophy won by Mrs. Adlam's dog, Ch. Raydium Brigadier, in 1937. Brigadier was eventually exported to the United States, where he became an important stud force at Mrs. Bennett's kennels.

There have now been eight Silverwood Trophy Competitions. Most breeders would agree that the competitions have been most successful in fulfilling their stated purpose—to stimulate the breeding of better Bull Terriers. At the first Silverwood there was excellent quality, for the winner, Ch. Killer Joe, and the Runner-Up, Ch. Midnight Melody, would still give today's best a run for their money. The most noticeable difference at the most recent competitions has been the *number* of quality animals. In 1970, Ch. Killer Joe dominated the Whites. He had no serious competition, for the Reserve Dog, Tantrum's Trad Lad, was merely a puppy. There were three good White bitches close enough in quality so that the referee was called upon to choose the Reserve. The scene in 1974 was far different. I was privileged to judge all of the classes at this show and found the line-up of White dogs and of White bitches simply breath-taking. There were twenty or more competitors in each class and so many good ones that no selection could be made at first glance. Many of these Bull Terriers have faults, for no one has yet bred a perfect dog, but the number and strength of their virtues is wonderful. With such superb animals as the foundation for future generations, the outlook, at least for White Bull Terriers, is very bright.

Similar progress has not been made in Coloreds. This is of grave concern to all interested in progress of the breed and has reopened the old controversy concerning the judging of Coloreds and Whites together. Although some of the most successful breeders in England have advised us to abandon the two-variety system, many U.S. breeders are not ready to do so.

Study of the results of the Silverwood Trophy Competitions will give a fairly good idea which kennels and breeders are producing top-flight Bull Terriers. There is a problem, however, in getting all of the outstanding dogs to the competition. Not every breeder with a good dog can travel from California or British Columbia to a show in Chicago or New York, nor can breeders in the East always manage to get away to a show a thousand or three thousand miles distant. This explains why each year the show is held at a different location.

Purpose of the Silverwood Competition is quoted as follows from the Purpose and Rules, 1974:

"The purpose of this competition is to bring together at one time and in one place America's outstanding Bull Terriers so their virtues may be assessed and appropriately recognized. In this situation breeders will have an opportunity to inspect America's top Bull Terriers and become acquainted with and talk to breeders from other sections of the country. They will be able to relate their own progress to the breed as a whole, and make decisions concerning future matings that should move the breed forward at an accelerated pace. It is hoped that through this activity better understanding and closer co-operation will develop throughout the entire Bull Terrier fancy."

In 1977, dogs eligible to compete were: 1. Best of Opposite Sex and Runner-Up of the 1976 competition. 2. All champions bred in North America. 3. Dogs placing as Winners Dog or Winners Bitch at a BTCA Specialty or Regional Specialty held after the 1976 Silverwood. 4. Qualifiers from Regional Qualifying Rounds. It seems that each year new regional clubs are being formed—a good indication of the increasing interest in Bull Terriers. Regional clubs currently recognized by the Bull Terrier Club of America to hold Regional Qualifying Rounds are: the Bull Terrier Club of New England, Knickerbocker Bull Terrier Club, Bull Terrier Club of Philadelphia, Garden State Bull Terrier Club, Golden Triangle Bull Terrier Club (Pittsburgh area), Fort Dearborn Bull Terrier Club, Golden State Bull Terrier Club (California), Bull Terrier Club of Canada, Bull Terrier Fanciers Association (Canada), Ottawa Valley Bull Terrier Club, Maritime Bull Terrier Club, and the Bull Terrier Club of Dallas. 5. The Board of Directors of the BTCA may invite an outstanding dog to compete.

Ch. Killer Joe, winner of first Silverwood Competition, 1970.

The results of the first eight Silverwood Trophy Competitions are as follows:

1970—Old Greenwich, Connecticut.

Judges, David Merriam and James Boland; *Referee,* Cecil Mann.

Best American Bred—Ch. Killer Joe by Ch. Krackton Robin of Wentwood ex Holcroft Kowhai Lottie by Souperlative Acetylene. Breeders-owners, Peggy and Michael Arnaud.

Runner-Up—Midnight Melody by Ch. Abraxas Ace of Aces ex Snowlady by Ch. Silverwood Signet. Breeder-owner, Charles Fleming.

Best of Opposite Sex—Midnight Melody.

Best White Bull Terrier—Ch. Killer Joe.

Best White Dog—Ch. Killer Joe.

Reserve White Dog—Tantrum's Trad Lad by Doonhamer's Maximillion ex Harper's Hemstitch by Souperlative Benbeau of Ormandy. Breeder-owner, Philip Hyde.

Best White Bitch—Ch. Belle Terre's Patience by Ch. Killer Joe ex Ch. Crestmere Bettina by Wilsmere Dauntless. Breeder-owner, H. Wm. Schmitz.

Reserve White Bitch—Ch. Holcroft Folly of Alaric by Ch. Krackton Robin of Wentwood ex Holcroft Kowhai Lottie by Souperlative Acetylene. Breeder, Peggy Arnaud. Owners, Michael Sottile and Alfred T. Bibby.

Best Colored Bull Terrier—Midnight Melody.

Best Colored Dog—Highland's Big Ben by Ch. Abraxas Ace of Aces ex Ch. Kearby Maywell's Gold Dust by Ch. White Squire of Scaramouche. Breeders-owners, Agnes and Forrest Rose.

Reserve Colored Dog—Ali Baba of High Knolls by Ch. Rough Rider of Monty-Ayr ex High Knoll of Monty-Ayr. Breeder-owner, John J. B. Jones.

Best Colored Bitch—Midnight Melody.

Reserve Colored Bitch—Ch. Aces Dynamite Galore by Ch. Abraxas Ace of Aces ex Ch. Pussy Galore by Ch. Ormandy's Ben of Highthorpe. Breeders, Ralph and Helen Bowles. Owners, Ralph Bowles and Carole Pettigrew.

1971—Ventura, California.

Judges, Colored Dogs, Alice Griffin and Oliver Ford; *Referee,* C. Mann. *Colored Bitches,* O. Ford and Marge Otis; *Referee,* Roy Johnson. *White Dogs,* Susan Meller and M. Otis; *Referee,* Norma Smith. *White Bitches,* N. Smith and Charles Meller; *Referee,* Dr.

Harry Otis. *Final Placings,* Cecil Mann and R. Johnson; *Referee,* C. Meller.

Best American Bred—Banbury Charity Buttercup by Targyt Silver Bob of Langville ex Charity Cyclamen by Ormandy's Souperlative Bar Sinister. Breeder-owner, Winkie Mackay-Smith.

Runner-Up—Banbury Briar (litter brother to Best American Bred). Owner, Winkie Mackay-Smith.

Best of Opposite Sex—Banbury Briar.

Best White Bull Terrier—Banbury Charity Buttercup.

Best White Dog—Banbury Briar.

Reserve White Dog—Ch. Tantrum's Trad Lad (see 1970 listings). Owner, Harvey Shames.

Best White Bitch—Banbury Charity Buttercup.

Reserve White Bitch—Ch. Alice Samoth Benbow by Ch. Goldfinger ex Broadside Frosty Mint Julep by Ch. Monkery's Mr. Frosty of Ormandy. Breeder, Thomas Moore. Owners, T. Moore and David Merriam.

Best Colored Bull Terrier—Ch. Carling's Minnie The Masher by Franda's Brandy Snap ex Polyanna of Monty-Ayr by Parade of Monty-Ayr. Breeders-owners, Carl and Ingrid Ackerman.

Best Colored Dog—Ch. Highland's Big Ben (see 1970 listing).

Reserve Colored Dog—Ch. Broadside Begone by Ch. Goldfinger ex Turney's Siren. Breeder-owner, David Merriam.

Best Colored Bitch—Ch. Carling's Minnie The Masher.

Reserve Colored Bitch—Turney's Nocturne by Ch. Abraxas Ace of Aces ex Cilla of Charlsdon. Breeder-owner, Fred Turney.

Ch. Banbury Charity Buttercup, owned by W. E. Mackay-Smith. 1971 Silverwood winner.

Can. and Am. Ch. Sunburst Solar System at nine months. 1972 Silverwood winner. Owned by Kathy and Len Spicer. Trophy presented by Douglas K. Rose to Kathy Spicer.

1972—Wheeling, Illinois.

Judges, Colored Dogs, Dr. Harry Otis and Marilyn Drewes; *Referee,* David Merriam. *Colored Bitches,* Dr. Otis and David Merriam; *Referee,* Marilyn Drewes. *White Dogs,* David Merriam and Dr. Otis; *Referee,* Carl Ackerman. *White Bitches,* Dr. Otis and Carl Ackerman; *Referee,* Norma Smith. Final Placings, Dr. Otis and Marilyn Drewes; *Referee,* David Merriam.

Best American Bred—Sunburst Solar System by Ch. Tantrum's Trad Lad ex Iella Desdamona by Ch. Monkery's Mr. Frosty of Ormandy. Breeder, Gary Travers. Owner, Len Spicer.

Runner-Up—Ch. Molyha Snip Snap Snorum by Ch. Abraxas Ace of Aces ex Huntress of Molyha by Ch. Oldlane's Pride. Breeder-owner, Mrs. Halina Molyneux.

Best of Opposite Sex—Ch. Highland's Big Ben (see 1970 listing).

Best White Bull Terrier—Sunburst Solar System.

Best White Dog—Ch. Tantrum's Trad Lad (see 1970 and 1971 listings).

Reserve White Dog—Paupens Mr. Wiggins by Ch. Maerdy Moonstone ex Romany Rock Rose by Romany Rockall. Breeder, J. Cowan. Owners, Paul and Penny Maier.

Best White Bitch—Sunburst Solar System.

Reserve White Bitch—Ch. Banbury Bountiful by Ch. Targyt Silver Bob of Langville ex Ch. Kashdowd Bounce by Romany Rover Scout. Breeder-owner, W. E. Mackay-Smith.

Best Colored Bull Terrier—Ch. Molyha Snip Snap Snorum.

Best Colored Dog—Ch. Highland's Big Ben.

Reserve Colored Dog—Ch. Belle Terre's Samson by Ch. Holcroft Diplomat ex Ch. Crestmere Bettina by Wilsmere's Dauntless. Breeder-owner, H. Wm. Schmitz.

Best Colored Bitch—Ch. Molyha Snip Snap Snorum.

Reserve Colored Bitch—Ch. Midnight Melody (see 1970 listing).

1973—Ambler, Pennsylvania.

Judges, Mrs. Mary Treen and Mr. Raymond Oppenheimer; *Referee, Colored Dogs,* Oliver Ford; *Referee, Colored Bitches,* M. Drewes.

Best American Bred—Paupens Mr. Wiggins by Ch. Maerdy Moonstone ex Romany Rock Rose by Romany Rockall. Breeder, J. Cowan. Owners, Paul and Penny Maier.

Runner-Up—Ch. Banbury Borealis by Ch. Banbury Briar ex Souperlative Meteor by Ch. Monkery's Mr. Frosty of Ormandy. Breeder, Mabel Smith. Owners, Alan and Marie Gerst.

Best of Opposite Sex—Carling's Goodness Gracious by Ch. Tantrum's Trad Lad ex Carling's Roseberry. Breeders, Ron Conti and Ingrid Ackerman. Owner, Edward Nentwich.

Best White Bull Terrier—Paupens Mr. Wiggins.

Best White Dog—Paupens Mr. Wiggins.

Reserve White Dog—Ch. Banbury Borealis.

Best White Bitch—Carling's Goodness Gracious.

Reserve White Bitch—Sunburst Solitaire by Ch. Tantrum's Trad Lad ex Iella Desdamona by Ch. Monkery's Mr. Frosty of Ormandy. Breeder-owner, Garry Travers.

Best Colored Bull Terrier—Regina of Colostaurus by Canadian Ch. Plaisance Seabryn Air Marshall ex Athena. Breeders, Mr. and Mrs. S. Fulljames. Owner, Gail Gordon.

Best Colored Dog—Ch. Highland's Big Ben (see 1970 listing).

Reserve Colored Dog—Ch. Ali Baba of High Knolls (see 1970 listing).

Best Colored Bitch—Regina of Colostaurus.

Reserve Colored Bitch—Ch. Molyha Snip Snap Snorum (see 1972 listing).

Can. Ch. Paupen's Mr. Wiggins, owned by Mr. and Mrs. Paul Maier. 1973 Silverwood winner.

1974—Youngstown, Ohio.

Judges, Colored Dogs and White Bitches, Marilyn Drewes and H. Wm. Schmitz; *Colored Bitches and White Dogs,* Marilyn Drewes and Marlin Mason; *Referee,* Cecil Mann.

Best American Bred—Banbury Bergerac by Ch. Targyt Silver Bob of Langville ex Ch. Harper's Hemstitch by Souperlative Benbeau of Ormandy. Breeder, Kenneth Newman. Owner, W. E. Mackay-Smith.

Runner-Up—Ch. Banbury Butter Rum by Ch. Trooper Duffy of Manchester ex Ch. Banbury Charity Buttercup by Ch. Targyt Silver Bob of Langville. Breeder, W. E. Mackay-Smith. Owner, Harvey Shames.

Best of Opposite Sex—Ch. Banbury Butter Rum.

Best White Bull Terrier—Banbury Bergerac.

Best White Dog—Banbury Bergerac.

Reserve White Dog—Ch. Banbury Beret by Banbury Bar None ex Valkyrie Kashdowd Clementina by Souperlative Slinger of Ormandy. Breeder-owner, W. E. Mackay-Smith.

Best White Bitch—Ch. Banbury Butter Rum.

Reserve White Bitch—Ch. Banbury Bouquet by Aricon's Acetylene of Banbury ex Ch. Kashdowd Bounce by Romany Rover Scout. Breeder-owner, W. E. Mackay-Smith.

Best Colored Bull Terrier—Ch. Dreadnaught's Top Deck by White Knight of Lenster ex Ch. Dreadnaught's Nemesis by Ch. Dreadnaught's Mr. Panda. Breeder, Betty Strickland. Owners, Earl and Charlene Rosinski.

Best Colored Dog—Ch. Dreadnaught's Top Deck.

Reserve Colored Dog—Canterbury's Taste of Honey by Ch.

Banbury Bergerac at fourteen months. 1974 Silverwood winner. Owned by W. E. Mackay-Smith.

Ch. Banbury Brass Tack of Maldon, 1975 Silverwood winner.

Canterbury's Mack The Knife ex Sweetie Pie. Breeder, Wm. Faith. Owner, Sophie Light.

Best Colored Bitch—Ch. Highland's Bashful Dwarf by Ch. Highland's Big Ben ex Highland's Lady Jessica by Ch. White Squire of Scaramouche. Breeder, Mary Rose. Owner, Wm. Weitz, Jr.

Reserve Colored Bitch—Canterbury's Dover Delite (litter sister to Canterbury's Taste of Honey). Breeder, Wm. Faith. Owners, David and Trudi Tamburri.

1975—Ventura, California.

Judges, Colored Dogs, Betty Strickland and Ray Williams; *Referee*, Ralph Bowles. *Colored Bitches and White Dogs*, Ralph Bowles and Betty Strickland; *Referee*, Ray Williams. *White Bitches*, Ralph Bowles and Ray Williams; *Referee*, Betty Strickland.

Best American Bred—Ch. Banbury Brass Tack of Maldon by Ch. Banbury Briar ex Banbury Butterfly by Ch. Trooper Duffy of Manchester. Breeders, Tom and Diane Griswold. Owners, Dr. John Blumberg and W. E. Mackay-Smith.

Runner-Up—Ch. Banbury Bouquet by Aricon's Acetylene of Banbury ex Ch. Kashdowd Bounce by Romany Rover Scout. Breeder-owner, W. E. Mackay-Smith.

Best of Opposite Sex—Ch. Banbury Bouquet.

Best White Bull Terrier—Ch. Banbury Brass Tack of Maldon.

Best White Dog—Ch. Banbury Brass Tack of Maldon.

Reserve White Dog—Magor Moonbear by Ch. Maerdy Moonstone ex Maerdy Manda. Breeders, Gordon and Norma Smith. Owner, Professor Ted Pyle.

Best White Bitch—Ch. Banbury Bouquet.

Reserve White Bitch—Banbury Backchat by Ch. Banbury Briar ex Ch. Kashdowd Bounce by Romany Rover Scout. Breeder, W. E. Mackay-Smith. Owners, Margaret Burns and W. E. Mackay-Smith.

Best Colored Bull Terrier—Ch. Griffwood's Jurisprudence by Ch. Souperlative Iceberg ex Broadside Samoth Rising Tide. Breeder, Virgil Griffith. Owners, Nigel and Christine Desmond.

Best Colored Dog—La Mirada's Wheel of Fortune by Ch. Valkyrie Ventura ex Flora Dora of La Mirada. Breeder, Susan Meller. Owner, Paul Turnbow.

Reserve Colored Dog—Ch. Campbell's Hey Jude of Barsoom by Ch. Abraxas Ace of Aces ex Cordova's Woola Barsoom. Breeders, Jean and Phil Glidewell. Owner, Brent L. Ruppel.

Best Colored Bitch—Ch. Griffwood's Jurisprudence.

Reserve Colored Bitch—Broadside Ring of Fire by Ch. Papilio Pop Music ex Ch. Rowdy Roxie. Breeder, David Merriam. Owner, Sharon Snider.

1976—Barrie, Ontario, Canada.

Judges, Carl Ackerman and Gail Gordon; *Referee,* Bill Morgan.

Best American Bred—Magor the Marquis by English and American Ch. Abraxas Achilles ex Ch. Maerdy Magdalene by English Ch. Abraxas Audacity. Breeders-owners, Gordon and Norma Smith.

Runner-Up—Ch. Chadwell's Chamaco by Ch. Banbury Briar ex Ch. Sunburst Solar System by Ch. Tantrum's Trad Lad. Breeders-owners, Len and Kathy Spicer.

Best of Opposite Sex—Ch. Banbury Backchat by Ch. Banbury Briar ex Ch. Kashdowd Bounce by Romany Rover Scout. Breeder, W. E. Mackay-Smith. Owners, W. E. Mackay-Smith and Margaret Burns.

Best White Bull Terrier—Magor the Marquis.

Best White Dog—Magor the Marquis.

Reserve White Dog—Chadwell's Chamaco.

Best White Bitch—Banbury Backchat.

Reserve White Bitch—Ch. Rapparree Vampirella by Canadian and American Ch. Tantrum's Trad Lad ex Ch. Banbury Butter Rum by Ch. Trooper Duffy of Manchester. Breeders-owners, Harvey and Paula Shames.

Best Colored Bull Terrier—Ch. Broadside Ring of Fire by Ch. Papilio Pop Music ex Ch. Rowdy Roxie by Ch. Goldfinger. Breeder, David Merriam. Owner, Sharon Snider.

Best Colored Dog—Bymarket Gunmetal Grenadier by Plaisance Seabryn Air Marshall ex Kashdowd Valkyrie Velvet. Breeder-owner, Bob Cole.

Reserve Colored Dog—Sunburst Spyfontein by Chadwell's Chamaco ex Sugarhill's Sunburst Starfire. Breeder, Gary Travers. Owners, Mr. and Mrs. Sam Brown.

Best Colored Bitch—Ch. Broadside Ring of Fire.

Reserve Colored Bitch—Treyacres Hi-Test Carnelian by Ch. Carnelian Golden Boy ex Carnelian Trinket. Breeder-owner, R. Jones.

1977—Northbrook, Illinois.

Judges, Colored Dogs, James Boland and Norma Smith; *Referee,* Irene Mann; Colored Bitches, Irene Mann and Norma Smith; *Referee,* James Boland; *White Dogs and Bitches,* James Boland and Irene Mann; *Referee,* Norma Smith; *Final Trophy Judging,* James Boland and Irene Mann; *Referee,* Norma Smith.

Best American Bred—Ch. St. Francis Gypsy Rover by English and American Ch. Abraxas Achilles ex Silverwood Swan Song by White Knight of Lenster. Breeder, Frank Foley. Owners, Frank Foley and Alex Shipley.

Runner-Up—Carling's Copperhead by Raparee Ragna ex Sugarhill's Lady in Satin by Ch. Arundela Cardinal. Breeder, Charles Cuccullo. Owner, Ingrid Ackerman.

Best of Opposite Sex—Carling's Copperhead.

Best White Bull Terrier—Ch. St. Francis Gypsy Rover.

Best White Dog—St. Francis Gypsy Rover.

Reserve White Dog—Ch. Banbury Bachelor's Button by Ch. Souperlative Silver Spoon ex Banbury Blossom by English and American Ch. Targyt Silver Bob of Langville. Breeder, W. E. Mackay-Smith. Owners, Margaret Burns and W. E. Mackay-Smith.

Best White Bitch—Ch. Tenacious Chadwell's Kelly Gay by Ch. Tantrum's Trad Lad ex Chadwell Nautical Girl by Ch. Banbury Briar. Breeder, Vicki McGrath. Owners, Len and Kathy Spicer.

Reserve White Bitch—Ch. Ragged Hill's Witchcraft by Ch. Ragged Hill's Worthy Sam ex Ragged Hill's Bloody Mary by Ch. Banbury Briar. Breeders, Peggy and Michael Arnaud. Owners, Peggy Arnaud and Drue King.

Best Colored Bull Terrier—Carling's Copperhead.

Best Colored Dog—Ch. The Duke of Goodwood by Ch. Plaisance Seabryn Air Marshall ex Molyha's Royal Casino. Breeders, Mr. and Mrs. T. Tierney. Owners, Mr. and Mrs. Brooke Wason.

Reserve Colored Dog—Ann-Dee's Red Adair by Ch. Paupens Mr. Wiggins ex Hollyfir's Copper Nob by English Ch. Hollyfir's Dog in a Doublet. Breeder, George Schreiber. Owners, Ron Angus and Elaine Bernard.

Best Colored Bitch—Carling's Copperhead.

Reserve Colored Bitch—Banbury Blaze of Glory by Ch. Souperlative Silver Spoon ex Sand Piper of Lenape. Breeder, Walter Rowland. Owner, W. E. Mackay-Smith.

Careful study of these Silverwood results can be very useful to the serious breeder. The same dogs appear over and over behind the best of today's young stock. Notice, too, that "like tends to beget like"—the Bull Terriers placing in the Silverwood are producing sons and daughters who also are earning top honors.

As a final thought, I suggest you look very carefully at the dams of the Silverwood winners. The better the bitch and her breeding, the better her chances of producing a real flyer!

Another highlight of the Silverwood weekend is the awarding of The Bar Sinister Trophy, a new award presented by James Maunde in honor of that most famous Bull Terrier, Ormandy Souperlative Bar Sinister. The trophy is awarded to a person who, in the opinion of a special committee appointed by the Bull Terrier Club of America, has done a great deal for the breed. Service to the breed may include many aspects such as breeding, judging, and writing, or any other activities which help Bull Terriers. The trophy, a solid bronze disk about ten inches in diameter and three-quarters of an inch thick, has a profile of Bar Sinister. Each year a new disk is cast for the new recipient of the award.

To date, the trophy has been awarded four times:

1974—To Irene Mann, diligent and self-sacrificing secretary of the Bull Terrier Club of America for many years.

1975—To Lindley Sutton, Delegate to The American Kennel Club from the Bull Terrier Club of America.

1976—To Alfred Bibby, long-time breeder and fancier who exemplifies the highest ethical standards and is particularly helpful to novices in the breed.

1977—To Douglas Rose, past president of the BTCA, who was directly responsible for organizing and administering the first few Silverwood Competitions.

Am. and Can. Ch. Tantrum's Trad Lad, sire of the 1972 Silverwood and 1973 Brigadier Trophy winners. Owned by Harvey and Paula Shames.

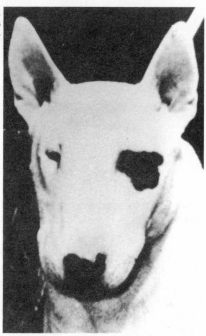

Can. and Am. Ch. Maerdy Moonstone, by Ch. Romany River Pirate ex Maerdy Moonrose. Owned by Mr. and Mrs. Gordon R. Smith.

Can. and Am. Ch. Maerdy Magdalene, by Ch. Abraxas Audacity ex Maerdy Mona, owned by Mr. and Mrs. Gordon R. Smith.

Bull Terriers in Canada

Presently there is a great resurgence of interest in Bull Terriers in Canada, where the breed at one time enjoyed great popularity. Back in the thirties, there were, in addition to The Bull Terrier Club of Canada, a Bull Terrier Club of Nova Scotia and a Bull Terrier Club of The Maritimes. After World War II, little was heard from Canadian breeders. Then, in 1970 when Mr. Oppenheimer came from England to judge the Bull Terrier Club of America Specialty, Bull Terriers appeared from everywhere! Among the incredible entry of one hundred three Bull Terriers were several outstanding Canadian dogs. In fact, the Canadians nearly swept the entire Specialty, taking Winners Bitch with Harper's Hemstitch, and Winners Dog and Best of Opposite Sex with Maerdy Moonstone. On the following day, the Canadians competed at the first Silverwood and took Reserve White Dog with the puppy Tantrum's Trad Lad. In the years since 1970, Canadian fanciers have attended and won many other Specialties. They have bred the Best White Bull Terriers at three Silverwood Competitions and the Best Colored Bull Terriers at two Silverwood Competitions, and definitely are very much a part of the Bull Terrier scene today. Among the active breed clubs in Canada are The Bull Terrier Club of Canada and The Bull Terrier Fancier's Association, both with headquarters in Ontario; the Ottawa Valley Bull Terrier Club; and the Maritime Bull Terrier Club.

Before briefly listing the major Canadian kennels, it might be worthwhile considering why, since 1970, Canadian breeders have had such good luck in producing excellent dogs. Perhaps it isn't just luck! Canadian breeders have imported several outstanding stud dogs, notably Ch. Maerdy Moonstone, a River Pirate son, and Ch. Plaisance Seabryn Air Marshall, a son of Langville Pilot Officer and therefore half brother to Silver Bob. But of greater significance is the fact that the Canadian breeders have brought in some excellent bitches, the real foundation of any successful breeding program. Among those lovely ladies were Harper's Hemstitch, Iella Desdamona, Kashdowd Sackville Sue, Romany Rock Rose,

Kashdowd Valkyrie Velvet, and Maerdy Magdalene. Four of these bitches have produced Silverwood Trophy winners. First, Hemstitch bred to an import, Doonhamers Maximillion, produced Tantrum's Trad Lad. Trad Lad bred to Iella Desdamona produced the 1972 Silverwood winner, Sunburst Solar System. Another Canadian-bred Trad Lad daughter, Ch. Tenacious Chadwell Kelly Gay, was Best White Bitch at the 1977 Silverwood Competition. Romany Rock Rose bred to Maerdy Moonstone produced the 1973 winner, Paupens Mr. Wiggins. Hemstitch, sold to Ken Newman in Pennsylvania, was bred to Mr. Newman's Targyt Silver Bob and produced the 1974 winner, Banbury Bergerac. Ch. Maerdy Magdalene bred to English and American Ch. Abraxas Achilles was the dam of the 1976 winner, Magor the Marquis. In 1972 and 1973, Canadians bred the top Colored Bull Terriers, Molyha Snip Snap Snorum and Regina of Colostaurus. Again in 1976 Canadians bred the Best Colored Dog, Bymarket Gunmetal Grenadier, and the Reserve Colored Dog, Sunburst Spyfontein. Again in 1977, Best Colored Dog, The Duke of Goodwood, was Canadian bred. In Canada as in England, Colored and Whites are not separated into different varieties but are shown together.

At the present time, the following kennels are actively breeding Bull Terriers:

Acmalta, owned by Mr. and Mrs. Bert Jackson in Acme, Alberta. The Jacksons have several good bitches such as Abraxas Another Asturia, litter sister to Achilles; Molyha Gold Card Mystery; and Canadian Ch. Storm's Spirited Sirius. They also have several dogs at stud—both imports and Canadian breds.

Aricon, owned by Mr. E. A. Stanley, seems to be a branch of Mr. Stanley's Aricon Kennels in England.

Avicorn, owned by Cornelius and Avice Dalke in Mission City, British Columbia. Imported stud dogs at Avicorn are Ch. Retsacnal Mystic and Geham Flying Officer.

Blencathra Bull Terriers are bred by Norm and Dianne Kent in Calgary, Alberta. Their foundation bitch is Ch. Kearby's Katarina, dam of Canadian and American Champions Blencathra's Warlord and Blencathra's Flossy Flake. Also interested in obedience work, the Kents have Avicorn's Charmaine Mystic, CD.

Bullseye is owned by Shelagh Kelsey in Dartmouth, Nova Scotia. Shelagh has the excellent White dog, Canadian Ch. Sackville Rowdy Man, and his sister, Canadian Ch. Sackville Supreme. These two champions are by Canadian Ch. Plaisance

Can. Ch. Plaisance Seabryn Air Marshall. Excellent expression. Owned by Joan Davidson and Gail Gordon.

Seabryn Air Marshall ex Ch. Kashdowd Sackville Sue. Rowdy Man has had an astounding show career in Canada, winning ten Group Firsts, twelve Group Seconds, ten Group Thirds, and nine Group Fourths. He also has his CD degree. Some dog! He and his sister have been shown serveral times as a brace—a rare phenomenon in the Bull Terrier world.

Bymarket is owned by Bob and Louise Cole in Ottawa. The Coles imported Canadian Ch. Hollyfir's Witch's Cub, a son of Ch. Romany River Pirate and Sweet Thursday of Hollyfir. Canadian Ch. Kashdowd Valkyrie Velvet, a brindle import, is also a resident of Bymarket. The Coles have bred Canadian Ch. Bymarket Boisterous Blanche and Bymarket Gunmetal Grenadier.

Chadwell, Reg., is the kennel of Len and Kathy Spicer in Saint Catharines, Ontario. The Spicers own the 1972 Silverwood winner, Ch. Sunburst Solar System. Bred to Ch. Banbury Briar, Solar System has produced a very good son, Ch. Chadwell's Chamaco. Also living at Chadwell is Trad Lad's litter sister Tantrum's Sweet Romance. Bred to a Trad Lad son, Ch. Carling's Marauder, Sweet Romance produced a nice bitch, Chadwell's Emma, who won the Knickerbocker Specialty in May 1974 under Judge Vera Sheridan Jackson. The Spicers also own the 1977 BTCA Specialty winner and 1977 Silverwood Best White Bitch, Ch. Tenacious Chadwell Kelly-Gay.

Magor is owned by Gordon and Norma Smith in Thunder Bay, Ontario. The Smiths imported Canadian and American Ch. Maerdy Moonstone, who was BOS at that famous 1970 Specialty Show where one hundred three dogs were entered under Mr. Oppenheimer. Moonstone is the sire of the 1973 Silverwood winner, Paupens Mr. Wiggins. The Smiths also have imported several lovely bitches including the Canadian and American Ch. Maerdy Magdalene, a daughter of Ch. Abraxas Audacity. She has twice won the Terrier Group and has placed in it numerous times. Bred to English and American Ch. Abraxas Achilles, she produced the 1976 Silverwood winner, Magor the Marquis.

Molyha is the name of Mrs. Halina Molyneux' Bull Terriers in Vancouver, British Columbia, the home of Ch. Molyha Snip Snap Snorum. Mrs. Molyneux imported the dog Oldlane's Pride, who sired Ch. Huntress of Molyha. When she was bred to Ch. Abraxas

Can. Ch. Hollyfir Witch's Cub, owned by Robert W. Cole.

Ace of Aces, Snip Snap ("Tiny") resulted. I expect that "Tiny" will produce some splendid offspring.

Oakstan in Woodstock, Ontario, is owned by Mr. and Mrs. Stan Oakley. They imported Geham St. Crispin and also own Ch. Oakstan Tom Collins.

Paupens in Winnipeg, Manitoba, is owned by Paul and Penny Maier. Their beloved pet is the 1973 Silverwood winner, Paupens Mr. Wiggins. Wiggins also won a Best in Show, all breeds, in Canada.

Piranha, owned by Gail Gordon, Joan Davidson, and Paul Wettlaufer, is one of the most active Bull Terrier kennels. Top dog at Piranha is Ch. Plaisance Seabryn Air Marshall, the first Bull Terrier to go Best in Show in Canada and the top Bull Terrier in Canada in 1971 and 1972. His son Ch. Sackville Rowdy Man and daughter Ch. Regina of Colostaurus are both Best-in-Show winners. Regina was the Best American Bred Colored Bull Terrier at the 1973 Silverwood Competition. Also at Piranha are Canadian Ch. Sadlewise Stearin, an import by Mr. Frosty, and Canadian Ch. Spartany Spirit of Satan, CD, a member of an all-breed obedience drill team!

Sackville, in Sackville, New Brunswick, is the prefix of Peter and Doreen Ide. Their imported bitch, Kashdowd Sackville Sue, when bred to Ch. Plaisance Seabryn Air Marshall, produced Champions Sackville Rowdy Man, Sackville Swamp Pirate, and Sackville Supreme.

Sunburst Bull Terriers are owned by Gary and Lynn Travers in Moffat, Ontario. The Travers are justifiably proud of their Mr. Frosty daughter, Canadian Ch. Iella Desdamona, Bull Terrier Brood Bitch of the year, 1973, according to *Terrier Type.* In her three litters she has produced eight champions: Solar System (1972 Silverwood winner), Strategy, Solitaire, Silver Scarab, Shotgun, Davidson's Storm, Snapdragon, and Sabateur.

Tantrum is the prefix used by Philip. and Gloria Hyde of Brampton, Ontario. The Hydes imported that great bitch, Canadian and American Ch. Harper's Hemstitch, dam of Ch. Tantrum's Trad Lad and Tantrum's Sweet Romance, and of Banbury Bergerac, the 1974 Silverwood winner who is now owned by the Hydes.

Venastra is the prefix of Mr. and Mrs. Nick Meesters of Collingwood, Ontario. Their best known dog is a brindle, Ch. Venastra's Son of Astronaut by Ch. Rombus Astronaut of Lenster.

Ch. La Mirada's Floral Dance, by Int. Ch. Comanche of Upend ex Gorgeous Gussy of La Mirada. Owned by Bob and Lynn Lawrence.

The Bull Terrier in the United States

The history of the Bull Terrier in our country shows how dependent we have always been on imported stock. Recognizing that the British dogs were superior, breeders over the years imported many animals, particularly stud dogs. There seemed to be a vain hope that a quality stud would compensate for most of the faults in the bitches sent him. Results of such breedings were usually disappointing, for the puppies tended to show many of "mother's" faults and few of "father's" virtues. The major problem was that the bitches were unrelated or so distantly related to the males that each breeding was pretty much an outcross. Since the parents were not from the same line, they were unlikely to be strong for the same virtues. Thus there was little chance of getting puppies of outstanding quality. As soon as a new import arrived, breeders would send their mediocre bitches to him with more disappointing results and very little progress for the breed. As a result of this rather haphazard sort of breeding, few lines were established which were strong for specific virtues.

An exception was the Monty-Ayr line established by Dr. Edward Montgomery in Pennsylvania. Starting with top quality English imports, Dr. Montgomery used intensive inbreeding to establish his own line of excellent Bull Terriers. That line is still going strong under the stewardship of the Mingo and Mingo East Kennels of the Masons and the Canterbury Kennels of the Tamburris. In California, James DeMangos is trying to establish an American line based on Monty-Ayr stock. Mrs. Jessie Bennett had also established a winning line by importing both dogs and bitches from Mrs. Adlam's Brendon Kennels. In the late fifties and early sixties, breeders began to import some good bitches so as to have more suitable mates for the imported stud dogs. When bred to dogs such as English and American Ch. Kowhai Uncle Bimbo, Ch. Krackton Robin of Wentwood, Ch. Swainhouse Sportsman, and Ch. Abraxas Ace of Aces, these bitches began to throw some high

Chadwell Chamaco at fourteen months. Owned by Kathy and Len Spicer.

Ch. Highland's Big Ben. Owner, Forrest Rose. Handler, John C. Kipp. Judge, Florise Hogan.

quality puppies. In the pedigrees of many of the best American dogs today you'll find names such as Romany Refresher, Wilsmeres Rosilla, Souperlative Spice of Heskethane, Valkyrie Milk Tray, Valkyrie White Clown, Meltdown Mark, Kowhai Fantasia, or Ormandy's Westward Ho—"ladies" important in raising the quality of our dogs.

So by the late sixties, things were looking up. Excellent imports were still arriving—Sturdee Wilsmere Christabelle, White Knight of Lenster, and Agates Mr. Pickwick at the Colkets; Targyt Silver Bob at Ken Neuman's; and Kashdowd Bounce at Winkie Mackay-Smith's. The breed had, in a sense, pulled itself up on its feet. The Silverwood Competitions have supplied the catalyst to get it up and away and moving forward by leaps and bounds!

Bull Terriers on the West Coast

Bejobos Kennels are a family hobby of Bob and Betty Cole of Portland, Oregon, and of their son John in Snohomish, Washington. The Coles own Ch. Uglee Pied Piper, a brindle import; American and Canadian Champions Bejobos Jack Frost and Bejobos Shinner, Ch. Bejobos Tough Guy, Ch. Bejobos Panda Bear, Ch. Bejobos Merry Sunshine, Ch. Avicorn's Corinthia Mystic, and three Canadian champions. The Coles are breeding both Coloreds and Whites.

Broadside Bull Terriers are owned by David C. Merriam in Upland, California. Dave has bred Champions Broadside Begone, Broadside Easy Come Easy Go, Turney's Bandit of Broadside, and Broadside Music Man. But Broadside is probably best known for its multitude of excellent imports, including Ch. Goldfinger, Ch. Ormandy's Bursons Bounty, Ch. Abraxas Antonius, Ch. Sadlewise Sandpiper, Ch. Valkyrie Moonmarble, Ch. Papilio Pop Music, and Ch. Souperlative Iceberg (co-owned until 1974). Most of these dogs have had dazzling show careers. Most important, however, is the fact that by making these English bloodlines available to American breeders, Dave is helping improve the breed as a whole.

Cordova Kennels of James DeMangos are unique in that there are no imports. Cordova stock is line bred to Monty-Ayr Bull Terriers primarily through Ch. Masterpiece of Monty-Ayr, a Best-in-Show winner, and Ch. Rough Rider of Monty-Ayr. Mr. DeMangos has bred the three champion sisters Cordova Tempest Storm, Frostine Elleon of Cordova, and Cordova Woola Barsoom, all of whom

Ch. Banbury Briar, owned by W. E. Mackay-Smith.

have produced champions. Another home-bred champion is Cordova Bona Roba.

Griffwood in Torrance, California, is the kennel prefix of Virgil Griffiths. Mr. Griffiths twice bred his bitch Broadside Samoth Rising Tide to Ch. Souperlative Iceberg. In the first litter was the outstanding brindle bitch, Ch. Griffwoods Jurisprudence. In the second litter was a lovely White dog, Ch. Griffwood's Calot of Nicrist.

La Mirada Kennels are probably the best known of the West

Ch. Monnie of Maerdy at nine months. Import owned by Holly Arthur—finished title at nine months.

Coast breeders. Charles and Susan Meller owned Ch. Swainhouse Sportsman and presently have Ch. Valkyrie Ventura, International Ch. Commanche of Upend, and Maerdy Montrose. To date, La Mirada has bred about forty champions! Much of this amazing success is probably due to the two excellent foundation bitches obtained from Al Bibby's Holcroft Kennels in Massachusetts. Ch. Holcroft Blossom was a beautiful brindle daughter of International Ch. Kowhai Uncle Bimbo ex Romany Refresher. The other bitch was Ch. Holcroft Kelly by Ch. Krackton Robin of Wentwood ex Holcroft Chorus Girl. Ch. La Mirada's Floral Dance is presently the top winning Colored Bull Terrier bitch in the United States. La Mirada is in Vista, California.

Maldon in Ontario, California, is owned by Tom and Diane Griswold, breeders of Ch. Lady Olivia of Maldon, Ch. Maldon Moon Mist, and the 1975 Silverwood winner, Ch. Banbury Brass Tack of Maldon.

Montara Bull Terriers in Gilroy, California, belong to Chuck and Suzanne Stacy. Although there are quite a few good animals in residence at Montara, probably the best known are the two brindle imports—Ch. Monkery Sea Link and his son, English Ch. Monkery Meltdown Sea Shanty.

Nicrist is the kennel name selected by Nigel and Chris Desmond of Canoga Park, California. Although the Desmonds have owned such successful show dogs as Ch. Hy-Lo's Mr. Ernie and Ch. Griffwoods Jurisprudence, by far their greatest winner has been Ch. Souperlative Iceberg. Some of his honors include forty-five Group placements; Top Bull Terrier sire of 1974 with nine published champions; and two Golden State Bull Terrier Club Specialty wins under Miss Graham-Weall and Jon Cole. Some dog!

Oyster Bay in Olympia, Washington, is owned by Lane and Carol Oppelt, who have bred a fine young dog, Ch. The Aristocrat of Oyster Bay.

Other California Bull Terriers will be found at *Wilton's* Kennels in El Cajon, where Colonel Wilbur Barnes is breeding Coloreds primarily. *Terriwood* Kennels of Janet and Aubrey Walker in Oxnard own the imported Ch. Booksale Doryman. *Angie B. Rose* in Lakewood owns American and Canadian Ch. Abraxas Astralboy, litter brother to the famed Audacity. Angie also owns Silverwood Spring Song, litter sister to Ch. Midnight Melody. There are many other enthusiastic Bull Terrier folk in California, where the Bull Terrier population has always been high.

Ch. Banbury Bouquet, owned by W. E. Mackay-Smith.

Ch. Nellie Bly of Ravenhill, owned by Rosalind Weiss.

Bull Terriers in the Southwest and the Rockies

Texas has, within the past four or five years, become a beehive of Bull Terrier activity, particularly in the Dallas area. The Bull Terrier Club of Dallas is a most enthusiastic group, and recently another club, the Southwestern Bull Terrier Club, has been formed, as well as another regional club, The Bull Terrier Club of Denver.

Cerberus, owned by Steve Schmidt, is in Carrollton, Texas. Steve has two White champions—Ch. Audax Scaramouche Nietzche and Ch. Banbury Buttermilk.

Dreadnaught is a well known Bull Terrier kennel formerly in the Midwest, but now in Tyler, Texas. Larry and Betty Strickland have bred thirteen champions, including Ch. Dreadnaught's Top Deck, best Colored Bull Terrier at the 1974 Silverwood Competition, Ch. Lord Cobbolt of Dreadnaught, Ch. Lady Nelle of Dreadnaught, Ch. Dreadnaught's Mr. Panda, Ch. Dreadnaught's Krackton Kwait and Ch. Dreadnaught's Krackton Kwick, Ch. Dreadnaught's Peppermint Pat, Ch. Dreadnaught's Sassy Brass, and others! Mr. Panda did a lot of winning in the East from 1966 through 1968, including several BTCA Specialties.

Rogues Row, owned by Gloria Holland in Oklahoma City, Oklahoma, has both Coloreds and Whites, including Champions Rogues Row Tacky Red Dress, Rogues Row Short Round, Rogues Row Snow Boots, Rogues Row Here's Lily, and Rogues Row Call Me Mister.

Tarlow Bull Terriers belong to Marvin and Mary Jane Tarlow in Dallas. They have bred Ch. Tarlow's Cleopatra, CD, who is going after her CDX degree next. The Tarlows have also bred Ch. Tarlow Fargo Blanchmange, Ch. Tarlow Wiggins Girl, and Ch. Tarlow Moonbonnet.

Bull Terriers in the South

Nashville, Tennessee, is home to some of the most important Bull Terriers in the United States. One of them, the lovely Ch. Midnight Melody, lives with her breeder-owner Charles Fleming. Not far away, at home with Ralph and Mary Bowles, are three English imports, English and American Ch. Abraxas Achilles, Regent Trophy winner in 1972, Agates Silver Tassie, and Harpers Hawkeye of Phidgity. Ralph also imported the late Ch. Abraxas Ace of Aces, a very successful show dog, winner of the Isis Vabo Trophy and many other honors including Best in Show. His real contribution to the breed was the number of fine offspring he pro-

Ch. Arundela Cardinal, owned by Dr. Jerald Schreiber.

Ch. Lady Jane of Sohnrize, by Ch. Dreadnaught's Mr. Panda ex Ch. Panda's Flame of Sohnrize, owned by Charlie Snyder.

duced. These include Ch. Agates Black Diamond (England), Agates Bronzino (another Isis Vabo winner), Ch. Highland's Big Ben, Ch. Molyha Snip Snap Snorum, Ch. Midnight Melody, Ch. Vicar's Robbit of Hy-Lo, and many others, for a total of twenty-three! Achilles ("Teddy") has been very busy at stud since his arrival in 1973, so his puppies are now appearing among the top competitors. He has sired the two most recent Silverwood winners, Magor the Marquis, who won in 1976, and St. Francis Gypsy Rover, who won in 1977.

Paradise Kennels owned by Charlie and Barbara Snyder are in Murray, Kentucky. The Snyders' first Bull Terriers were Ch. Lady Jane of Sohnrise, Ch. Panda's Flame of Sohnrise, and Ch. Panda's Slasher of Sohnrise. They now have a very good stud dog, Aricon's Acetylene of Banbury, sire of the Reserve White Bitch at the 1974 Silverwood Competition, Ch. Banbury Bouquet.

Onslaut, Reg., Bull Terriers are bred by Fred and Germaine Welsh in Alva, Florida. Over the years, the Welshes have bred about ten champions, including Ch. Onslaught's Scaramouche, Ch. Sir William of Onslaught, Ch. Suzan of Onslaught, Ch. White Diamond of Onslaught, and several others. Ch. Onslaught's David appeared for two years on Broadway playing the part of "Bullseye" in the musical production *Oliver!* Although David's role was critical, for he had to walk along by himself, turn at just the right place, and nose out the murderer, Sikes, his performance was always flawless!

Bull Terriers in the Midwest

There are a great many active breeders in this part of the country. Unfortunately, space does not permit listing everyone and all of their good dogs.

Ann-Dees in Washington, Pennsylvania, is the kennel prefix of Elaine Bernard and Betty Desmond. Elaine has bred some really excellent Bull Terriers, including Ch. Lady Ann Dee's Julie; Julie's son, Christopher Robin; and a lovely fawn bitch, Ch. Lady Ann Dee's Mirical Girl.

Barclay, owned by Kimball E. Harter of Winnetka, Illinois, is home to Ch. Barclay's Algonquin Queen and Ch. Dreadnaught's Krackton Kwick, CD.

Brandy Bull Terriers belong to Robert and Mary Vargo in Akron, Ohio. Highland's Sneezy Dwarf and her daughter Brandy's Encore are the foundation bitches for the Vargos' breeding program. Sneezy produced a very good son, Brandy's Apple Jack.

Bristol Bull Terriers are owned by Mr. and Mrs. Bobbie Spencer of Yorkville, Illinois. Their foundation bitch is Highland's April Love, BTCA Specialty winner in 1972, a lovely little thing who should give them excellent puppies.

Canterbury Kennels in Gibsonia, Pennsylvania, are not really in the Midwest, but are so close to Ohio that I am including them here. Dave and Trudi Tamburri have been breeding Bull Terriers of Monty-Ayr bloodlines. Their Ch. Canterbury's Mack the Knife has proven himself a crack stud dog siring many champions. Both the Reserve Colored Dog and Bitch at the 1974 Silverwood were sired by Mack, who is, by the way, a White dog.

Haltbar in Lansing, Michigan, is the home of the brindle import, Ch. Monkery Sea Boots, proudly owned by Carl and Barbara Pew. Sea Boots has had and is still having a fantastic show career. Not knowing what his final tally will be, it suffices to say that in early 1977 he had four Best-in-Show wins and had placed in approximately sixty Groups!

Highland's Bull Terriers' most famous son is Ch. Highland's Big Ben, bred by Forrest and Agnes Rose in Highland Park, Illinois. I doubt if any other American Bred Colored dog has had such an astounding show career, including two Best-in-Show awards at all-breed shows. He has won BOV at eight Specialties, and was Best Colored Dog at the Silverwood for four years in a row and BOS in 1972 to win the Brigadier Trophy. Of greater importance to the breed, however, is the beautiful litter he sired in 1971—the famous Seven Dwarf litter which contained several excellent Bull Terriers, including Ch. Highland's Bashful Dwarf, winner of two Specialties and Best Colored Bitch at the 1974 Silverwood. Another litter of Ben's contained the 1972 BTCA Specialty winner, Ch. Highland's April Love. The Roses do have other dogs, including Champions Kearby Maywell's Golddust, Highland's Constant Harp, White Squire of Scaramouche, and Kearby's Highland Lass.

Intrepid, in Northfield, Illinois, belongs to Bob and Anita Bartell. Ch. Lord Downey of Dreadnaught, and several other champions co-owned with Betty Strickland of Dreadnaught comprise the Bull Terrier forces at Intrepid.

Bull Terriers of Melrose are proudly bred by Douglas K. Rose, Past President of the Bull Terrier Club of America. Melrose breeds medium-sized dogs, some of the best being Ch. Lady Guinevere of Melrose, Ch. Sir Brian of Melrose, and Ch. Benchmark of Melrose, WD at two Specialties and at Westminster in

Ch. Banbury Butter Rum, owned by
Harvey Shames.

Ch. Banbury Beret, owned by W. E. Mackay-Smith.

1974. His dam, Tres Petite of Melrose, is a lovely Killer Joe daughter who should have completed her championship. Bull Terriers of Melrose are now located in Vermillion, South Dakota.

Pendragon is the new kennel name for breeders Holly Arthur and Nancy Van Heule in Riverwoods, Illinois. Originally *Scaramouche,* the name was changed when the owners decided to phase out their American bred stock gradually and start again with English imports. To date they have imported Ch. Monnie of Maerdy, Ch. Maerdy Moustachio, and Maerdy Manny, all beautifully bred Bull Terriers. This kennel is breeding both Coloreds and Whites, having produced many champions of all colors in the past— including Ch. White Squire of Scaramouche, Ch. Scaramouche's Babe, and Ch. Pendragon's Knight Templar.

Tornado's in Omaha, Nebraska, is owned by Earl Van Wie. Tornado has produced quite a few champions, including Tornado's Mr. Rocky.

Bull Terriers in the East

There are so many important kennels in this part of the country that it would take an entire book to cover them adequately. I will try to list those which have been in the past or are now in the present most active in the breed.

Alaric Bull Terriers in Somerville, New Jersey, are owned by Mr. and Mrs. Michael Sottile. Their imported Ch. Franda's Brandy Snap sired six champions, including Ch. Carling's Minnie the Masher, Best Colored Bull Terrier at the 1971 Silverwood. Alaric owns Ch. Holcroft Folly of Alaric, Reserve at the 1970 Silverwood. A son of Folly's is Ch. Holcroft White Devil.

Banbury Cross in Coatesville, Pennsylvania, is owned by W. E. Mackay-Smith. If you look at the results of the 1974 Silverwood, you will find that all four winners in Whites were Banbury Bull Terriers! This kennel is, in my opinion, the leading breeding kennel in the United States today. Winkie's first import, Ch. Kashdowd Bounce, won five Specialties, including the 1970 Ox Ridge show where one hundred three Bull Terriers were entered. Bounce has produced seven champions to date. At least thirty champions bear the Banbury prefix, and the number is steadily increasing. These dogs have won all sorts of honors and are showing by their progeny the importance of good breeding. Litter sister and brother Ch. Banbury Charity Buttercup and Ch. Banbury

Briar were Winner and Runner-Up at the 1971 Silverwood. Briar's son, Ch. Banbury Borealis, was Runner-Up at the 1973 Silverwood, and his son Chamaco and daughter Backchat were Runner-Up and Best of Opposite Sex at the 1976 Silverwood. Buttercup's daughter, Ch. Banbury Butter Rum, was Runner-Up at the 1974 Silverwood, and Butter Rum's daughter, Rapparee Vampirella, was Reserve White Bitch at the 1976 event. The Banbury line has been developed from Ch. Targyt Silver Bob of Langville and the Bar Sinister daughter, Charity Cyclamen. It was a tragedy that the lovely Bounce daughter, Ch. Banbury Bountiful, required emergency surgery and could never be bred. In addition to Briar, Ch. Souperlative Silver Spoon is also at stud at Banbury.

Belle Terre Bull Terriers are bred by Bill and Nancy Schmitz in Port Jefferson, New York. Their foundation bitch, Ch. Crestmere Bettina, produced Ch. Belle Terre's Samson when bred to Ch. Holcroft Diplomat and Ch. Belle Terre's Patience when bred to Ch. Killer Joe. Both Samson and Patience have placed at Silverwood Competitions. Other home-bred champions include Ch. Belle Terre's Bring Down, Belle Terre's Squeeze Me, and Ch. Belle Terre's White Heat. Bill was President of the Bull Terrier Club of America from 1975 to 1977.

Bedford in Old Greenwich, Connecticut, is owned by Oliver Ford, a long-time fancier and Past President of the BTCA. Mr. Ford imported Ch. Meltdown Mark, a daughter of Ch. Ormandy's Ben of Highthorpe. "Marky" was a Specialty winner who produced some excellent puppies, such as Ch. Crestmere Silver Ben.

Borealis in Huntington, New York, is the home of Ch. Banbury Borealis ("Henry"), owned by Allan and Marie Gerst. Runner-Up in the 1973 Silverwood, "Henry" has won six Specialties and numerous other supported shows. He is by Ch. Banbury Briar ex Souperlative Meteor, a Mr. Frosty daughter.

Boatswain in Fort Loudon, Pennsylvania, is the prefix of Steve and Brenda Weintraub. Just getting started in the breed, the Weintraubs have two champions, Ch. Franda Carling Clipper and Ch. Banbury Bella, a "Bounce" daughter.

Carnelian is Cassie Bouton's kennel in Greenport, Long Island, New York. Cassie "rescued" Ch. Dreadnaught's Mr. Panda and had him for over four years until his death in 1973. Panda's last litter included two very good puppies—Ch. Carnelian Golden Boy, a fawn smut proving solid for color, and Ch. Kismet of Carnelian, WB at the Philadelphia Specialty judged by Mrs. Sweeten in 1973. Other home-bred champions include Prince Charles, Duke of

Ch. Souperlative Iceberg, owned by Nigel and Chris Desmond.

Ch. Holcroft Diplomat, owned by Carl and Ingrid Ackerman.

Windsor, and Beloved Rogue, with many more well on the way!

Carlings, now in Upper Black Eddy, Pennsylvania, is a very successful kennel owned by Carl and Ingrid Ackerman. Their original foundation bitch, Polyanna of Monty-Ayr, is behind just about all of their present stock. "Polly" produced Ch. Carling's Minnie the Masher, Ch. Carling's Solitaire, Ch. Carling's Flower Power, Ch. Carling's Rocky Jacco, and Ch. Carling's Marauder. In 1968, Carlings purchased Ch. Holcroft Diplomat, who sired Solitaire, Ch. Belle Terre's Samson, Ch. Carling's Ambassador, and Ch. Lavender's Chippewa Squaw, dam of Ch. Lavender's Robinhood. The Ackermans have at stud Rapparee Ragna, a Trad Lad son, who sired Carling's Copperhead, Runner-up, Best of Opposite Sex, and Best Colored at the 1977 Silverwood. Loose together in the house at all times are the Bull Terriers "Polly" and "Gus," a Siamese cat, "Trixie" (a Yorkie), and "Boris" (an ancient Basset).

Crestmere is the prefix of Cecil and Irene Mann in Newburgh, New York. Cecil is a Past President of the BTCA, and Irene was Secretary of that organization for many years. Crestmere has owned several important English imports such as Ch. Wilsmere Rosilla, Wilsmere's Dauntless, and Ch. Souperlative Spice of Heskethane. At stud are a Silver Bob son, Crestmere Esthetic Echo; Echo's son, Ch. Silver Ben; Crestmere Fair Trade, a Ventura son; and Crestmere Dan Patch, a Briar son.

Domino, owned by Charles and Rosalind Clamper, and *Ravenhill,* owned by Jay Coupe, are in Philadelphia. These breeders have co-operated in the breeding and ownership of Ch. Nellie Bly of Ravenhill, Ch. D'Artagnan of Ravenhill, and Ch. Gentle Annie of Ravenhill. And the Clampers have bred Ch. Domino's Ramblin' Man.

Holcroft Kennels, formerly in Lynnfield, Massachusetts, and now relocated in New Hampshire, have been breeding Bull Terriers for over thirty years. Al Bibby has contributed a great deal to the breed through his top imported stud dogs, English and American Ch. Kowhai Uncle Bimbo and Ch. Krackton Robin of Wentwood. When the Colkets died, Al took White Knight of Lenster to Holcroft, where this Bar Sinister son was at stud until his death in 1976. He sired close to twenty champions, passing on his superb temperament and great substance, both well illustrated by his son, Ch. The Duke of Holcroft. One of the most important bitches ever imported to the United States was Kowhai Fantasia, who arrived at Holcroft already in whelp to Souperlative Acetylene. In the resulting litter were Holcroft Hurricane, Holcroft Silver Queen, and Holcroft Kowhai Lottie. Although none of these was shown to a championship, each produced champions and they are in the pedigrees of many of today's best dogs. Holcroft Kowhai Lottie became the Arnaud's foundation bitch and the dam of five champions, including Ch. Killer Joe. A few of the other fine dogs bred at Holcroft were Champions Holcroft Blossom, Holcroft Kelly, Holcroft Dawn of Tomorrow, Holcroft Diplomat, and Holcroft Lady Joan.

Lochreggand Kennels of Mary Andregg in Sheffield, Massachusetts, is the home of Ch. Lavender's Robinhood, the best Bull Terrier ever bred by the late Lavender Lovell. Robinhood, a huge and handsome brindle and white son of Ch. Roughrider of Monty-Ayr, has had a very successful show career with Specialty wins and Group placements galore.

Mingo East belongs to Mardy Mason of Newtown Square, Pennsylvania. Mardy is continuing the Mingo Kennels owned by his father, the late Joseph Mason. Mingo Bull Terriers are bred from the best of the Monty-Ayr stock and have produced such well known dogs as Ch. Aquarius of Mingo, a Best-in-Show winner.

Mystero is owned by Jim Boland on Staten Island, New York. His best bitch was probably Ch. Sturdee Wilsmere Christabelle, a Thunderflash daughter who completed her championship by winning three five-point shows in a row. Jim has been in the breed for many years and in the past bred Ch. Tim Buck II, Ch. Aesop, Ch. Mystero Charmaine, and Ch. Mystero Brady.

Nippy's is the prefix chosen by Marilyn Drewes in Wenham, Massachusetts, in honor of her first Bull Terrier, Ch. Holcroft Queenie's Nippy Girl, dam of Ch. Nippy's Silver Duchess, Ch. Nippy's Steven The Sea Dog, and Ch. Nippy's Salty Finale—all by White Knight of Lenster. Salty produced two nice daughters to Harper's Hawkeye of Phidgity — Ch. Nippy's Salty Rose and Nippy's Daisy of Holcroft.

Ragged Hill in West Brookfield, Massachusetts, is the home of the first Silverwood winner, Ch. Killer Joe, and his breeders-owners Peggy and Michael Arnaud. Their foundation bitch, "Crikey," officially known as Holcroft Kowhai Lottie, produced three champions by Ch. Krackton Robin of Wentwood—Killer Joe, Holcroft Archer, and Holcroft Folly of Alaric—and two champions by White Knight of Lenster—Ragged Hill's I Am Curious and

Trooper Duffy of Manchester. Duffy sired three champions in his first litter, one of them being the 1974 Runner-Up at the Silverwood Competition, Ch. Banbury Butter Rum. Yet he has been used at stud only twice since, possibly because he lives as a house pet in New Hampshire and breeders have forgotten that he exists! Other Ragged Hill champions include Ch. Ragged Hill's Devastation, Ch. Briarbrooks Terrathustra, Ch. Ragged Hill's Worthy Sam, Ch. Ragged Hill's Witchcraft, and Ch. Ragged Hill's Aurora.

Rapparee is owned by Harvey and Paula Shames in Sugar Loaf, New York. The Shames purchased Ch. Tantrum's Trad Lad from Phil Hyde in Canada. Perusal of the Silverwood results will indicate what an important stud force Trad Lad was. His most famous offspring are the 1972 Silverwood winner, Ch. Sunburst Solar System; her sister Ch. Sunburst Solitaire; Ch. Carling's Marauder; the 1973 Silverwood Best White Bitch, Ch. Carling's Goodness Gracious; the 1976 Silverwood Reserve White Bitch, Rapparee Vampirella; and Ch. Tenacious Chadwell Kelly-Gay. Trad Lad was Best White Dog at the 1972 Silverwood. His accidental death in 1976 was a great loss to the breed, for he sired truly excellent daughters. The Shames also own Ch. Banbury Butter Rum, Runner-Up at the 1974 Silverwood and dam of Vampirella.

Sugarhill is a new kennel owned by Dr. Jerald Schreiber in Farmingdale, New Jersey. Ch. Arundela Cardinal, a River Pirate son, has done a lot of winning, ranking as Number Two Colored Bull Terrier for 1974, Phillips System.

Shiloh Bull Terriers will be found with owners Joy and Glenn Mullins in Doswell, Virginia. The Mullinses own Ch. Bridgit of Nottingham and have bred Ch. Shiloh's Fidgity Gidgit.

Winsted in Winsted, Connecticut, is famous for obedience trained Bull Terriers coached by Dr. Harry Otis and Marge Otis. Recently a fair number of people have trained their Bull Terriers to CD degrees, but Harry and Marge were doing obedience work when no one else was interested! Over the years they have trained Winsted's Bedford Belle, UDT; Ch. Bedford's Lady Penelope, TD; Ch. Bedford's Top Hat, CD; Winsted Michelle, CDX; and Wilsmere Pixie of Paladium, CD. If anyone doubts the versatility of the Bull Terrier, show them those two Tracking Dog degrees!

Zodiac is the kennel of George Schreiber, Montclair, New Jersey. George imported a red, Hollyfir's Copper Nob, and a brindle, Esse's Countess, in whelp to Souperlative Sunstar. In the resulting litter was a tricolor champion, Signature's Black Bart.

Ch. Belle Terre's Squeeze Me, owned by H. Wm. Schmitz.

The Duke of Holcroft (White Knight of Lenster ex Belle Terre's Miss Hannah) at twelve months. Owned by Tom Fitzgibbon and Alfred T. Bibby.

Manners for the Family Dog

Although each dog has personality quirks and idiosyncrasies that set him apart as an individual, dogs in general have two characteristics that can be utilized to advantage in training. The first is the dog's strong desire to please, which has been built up through centuries of association with man. The second lies in the innate quality of the dog's mentality. It has been proved conclusively that while dogs have reasoning power, their learning ability is based on a direct association of cause and effect, so that they willingly repeat acts that bring pleasant results and discontinue acts that bring unpleasant results. Hence, to take fullest advantage of a dog's abilities, the trainer must make sure the dog understands a command, and then reward him when he obeys and correct him when he does wrong.

Commands should be as short as possible and should be repeated in the same way, day after day. Saying "Heel," one day, and "Come here and heel," the next will confuse the dog. *Heel, sit, stand, stay, down,* and *come* are standard terminology, and are preferable for a dog that may later be given advanced training.

Tone of voice is important, too. For instance, a coaxing tone helps cajole a young puppy into trying something new. Once an exercise is mastered, commands given in a firm, matter-of-fact voice give the dog confidence in his own ability. Praise, expressed in an exuberant tone, will tell the dog quite clearly that he has earned his master's approval. On the other hand, a firm "No" indicates with equal clarity that he has done wrong.

Rewards for good performance may consist simply of praising lavishly and petting the dog, although many professional trainers use bits of food as rewards. Tidbits are effective only if the dog is hungry, of course. And if you smoke, you must be sure to wash your hands before each training session, for the odor of nicotine is repulsive to dogs. On the hands of a heavy smoker, the odor of nicotine may be so strong that the dog is unable to smell the tidbit.

Correction for wrong-doing should be limited to repeating "No," in a scolding tone of voice or to confining the dog to his bed. Spanking or striking the dog is taboo—particularly using sticks, which might cause injury, but the hand should never be used either. For field training as well as some obedience work, the hand is used to signal the dog. Dogs that have been punished by slapping have a tendency to cringe whenever they see a hand raised and consequently do not respond promptly when the owner's intent is not to punish but to signal.

Some trainers recommend correcting the dog by whacking him with a rolled-up newspaper. The idea is that the newspaper will not injure the dog but that the resulting noise will condition the dog to avoid repeating the act that seemingly caused the noise. Many authorities object to this type of correction, for it may result in the dog's becoming "noise-shy"—a decided disadvantage with show dogs which must maintain poise in adverse, often noisy, situations. "Noise-shyness" is also an unfortunate reaction in field dogs, since it may lead to gun-shyness.

To be effective, correction must be administered immediately, so that in the dog's mind there is a direct connection between his act and the correction. You can make voice corrections under almost any circumstances, but you must never call the dog to you and then correct him, or he will associate the correction with the fact that he has come and will become reluctant to respond. If the dog is at a distance and doing something he shouldn't, go to him and scold him while he is still involved in wrong-doing. If this is impossible, ignore the offense until he repeats it. Then correct him properly.

Especially while a dog is young, he should be watched closely and stopped before he gets into mischief. All dogs need to do a certain amount of chewing, so to prevent your puppy's chewing something you value, provide him with his own balls and toys. Never allow him to chew cast-off slippers and then expect him to differentiate between cast-off items and those you value. Nylon stockings, wooden articles, and various other items may cause intestinal obstructions if the dog chews and swallows them, and death may result. Rubber and plastic toys may also be harmful if they are of types the dog can bite through or chew into pieces and then swallow. So it is essential that the dog be permitted to chew only on bones or toys he cannot chew up and swallow.

Serious training for obedience should not be started until a dog is a year old. But basic training in house manners should begin the day the puppy enters his new home. A puppy should never be given the run of the house but should be confined to a box or small pen except for play periods when you can devote full attention to him. The first thing to teach the dog is his name, so that whenever he hears it, he will immediately come to attention. Whenever you are near his box, talk to him, using his name repeatedly. During play periods, talk to him, pet him, and handle him, for he must be conditioned so he will not object to being handled by a veterinarian, show judge, or family friend. As the dog investigates his surroundings, watch him carefully and if he tries something he shouldn't, reprimand him with a scolding "No!" If he repeats the offense, scold him and confine him to his box, then praise him. Discipline must be prompt, consistent, and always followed with praise. Never tease the dog, and never allow others to do so. Kindness and understanding are essential to a pleasant, mutually rewarding relationship.

When the puppy is two to three months old, secure a flat, narrow leather collar and have him start wearing it (never use a harness, which will encourage tugging and pulling). After a week or so, attach a light leather lead to the collar during play sessions and let the puppy walk around, dragging the lead behind him. Then start holding the end of the lead and coaxing the puppy to come to you. He will then be fully accustomed to collar and lead when you start taking him outside while he is being housebroken.

Housebreaking can be accomplished in a matter of approximately two weeks provided you wait until the dog is mature enough to have some control over bodily functions. This is usually at about four months. Until that time, the puppy should spend most of his day confined to his penned area, with the floor covered with several thicknesses of newspapers so that he may relieve himself when necessary without damage to floors.

Either of two methods works well in housebreaking—the choice depending upon where you live. If you live in a house with a readily accessible yard, you will probably want to train the puppy from the beginning to go outdoors. If you live in an apartment without easy access to a yard, you may decide to train him first to relieve himself on newspapers and then when he has learned control, to teach the puppy to go outdoors.

If you decide to train the puppy by taking him outdoors, arrange some means of confining him indoors where you can watch him closely—in a small penned area, or tied to a short lead (five or six feet). Dogs are naturally clean animals, reluctant to soil their quarters, and confining the puppy to a limited area will encourage him to avoid making a mess.

A young puppy must be taken out often, so watch your puppy closely and if he indicates he is about to relieve himself, take him out at once. If he has an accident, scold him and take him out so he will associate the act of going outside with the need to relieve himself. Always take the puppy out within an hour after meals—preferably to the same place each time—and make sure he relieves himself before you return him to the house. Restrict his water for two hours before bedtime and take him out just before you retire for the night. When you wake in the morning, take him out again.

For paper training, set aside a particular room and cover a large area of the floor with several thicknesses of newspapers. Confine the dog on a short leash and each time he relieves himself, remove the soiled papers and replace them with clean ones.

As his control increases, gradually decrease the paper area, leaving part of the floor bare. If he uses the bare floor, scold him mildly and put him on the papers, letting him know that there is where he is to relieve himself. As he comes to understand the idea, increase the bare area until papers cover only space equal to approximately two full newspaper sheets. Keep him using the papers, but begin taking him out on a leash at the times of day that he habitually relieves himself. Watch him closely when he is indoors and at the first sign that he needs to go, take him outdoors. With this method too, restrict the puppy's water for two hours before bedtime, but if necessary, permit him to use the papers before you retire for the night.

Using either method, the puppy will be housebroken in an amazingly short time. Once he has learned control he will need to relieve himself only four or five times a day.

Informal obedience training, started at the age of about six to eight months, will provide a good background for any advanced training you may decide to give your dog later. The collar most effective for training is the metal chain-link variety. The correct size for your dog will be about one inch longer than the measurement around the largest part of his head. The chain must be slipped through one of the rings so the collar forms a loop. The collar should be put on with the loose ring at the right of the dog's neck, the chain attached to it coming over the neck and through the holding ring, rather than under the neck. Since the dog is to be at your left for most of the training, this makes the collar most effective.

The leash should be attached to the loose ring, and should be either webbing or leather, six feet long and a half inch to a full inch

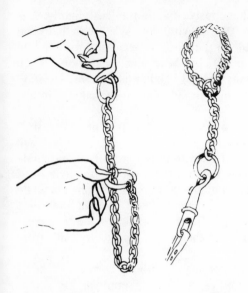

Chain-link collar. The collar should be removed whenever the dog is not under your immediate supervision, for many dogs have met death by strangulation when a collar was left on and became entangled in some object.

wide. When you want your dog's attention, or wish to correct him, give a light, quick pull on the leash, which will momentarily tighten the collar about the neck. Release the pressure instantly, and the correction will have been made. If the puppy is already accustomed to a leather collar, he will adjust easily to the training collar. But before you start training sessions, practice walking with the dog until he responds readily when you increase tension on the leash.

Set aside a period of fifteen minutes, once or twice a day, for regular training sessions, and train in a place where there will be no distractions. Teach only one exercise at a time, making sure the dog has mastered it before going on to another. It will probably take at least a week for the dog to master each exercise. As training progresses, start each session by reviewing exercises the dog has already learned, then go on to the new exercise for a period of concerted practice. When discipline is required, make the correction immediately, and always praise the dog after corrections as well as when he obeys promptly. During each session stick strictly to business. Afterwards, take time to play with the dog.

The first exercise to teach is heeling. Have the dog at your left and hold the leash as shown in the illustration on the preceding page. Start walking, and just as you put your foot forward for the first step, say your dog's name to get his attention, followed by the

133

command, "Heel!" Simultaneously, pull on the leash lightly. As you walk, try to keep the dog at your left side, with his head alongside your left leg. Pull on the leash as necessary to urge him forward or back, to right or left, but keep him in position. Each time you pull on the leash, say "Heel!" and praise the dog lavishly. When the dog heels properly in a straight line, start making circles, turning corners, etc.

Once the dog has learned to heel well, start teaching the "sit." Each time you stop while heeling, command "Sit!" The dog will be at your left, so use your left hand to press on his rear and guide him to a sitting position, while you use the leash in your right hand to keep his head up. Hold him in position for a few moments while you praise him, then give the command to heel. Walk a few steps, stop, and repeat the procedure. Before long he will automatically sit whenever you stop. You can then teach the dog to "sit" from any position.

When the dog will sit on command without correction, he is ready to learn to stay until you release him. Simply sit him, command "Stay!" and hold him in position for perhaps half a minute, repeating "Stay," if he attempts to stand. You can release him by saying "O.K." Gradually increase the time until he will stay on command for three or four minutes.

The "stand-stay" should also be taught when the dog is on leash. While you are heeling, stop and give the command "Stand!" Keep the dog from sitting by quickly placing your left arm under him, immediately in front of his right hind leg. If he continues to try to sit, don't scold him but start up again with the heel command, walk a few steps, and stop again, repeating the stand command and preventing the dog from sitting. Once the dog has mastered the stand, teach him to stay by holding him in position and repeating the word "Stay!"

The "down stay" will prove beneficial in many situations, but especially if you wish to take your dog in the car without confining him to a crate. To teach the "down," have the dog sitting at your side with collar and leash on. If he is a large dog, step forward with the leash in your hand and turn so you face him. Let the leash touch the floor, then step over it with your right foot so it is under the instep of your shoe. Grasping the leash low down with both hands, slowly pull up, saying, "Down!" Hold the leash taut until the dog goes down. Once he responds well, teach the dog to stay in the down position (the down-stay), using the same method as for the sit- and stand-stays.

To teach small dogs the "down," another method may be used. Have the dog sit at your side, then kneel beside him. Reach across his back with your left arm, and take hold of his left front leg close to the body. At the same time, with your right hand take hold of his right front leg close to his body. As you command "Down!" gently lift the legs and place the dog in the down position. Release your hold on his legs and slide your left hand onto his back, repeating, "Down, stay," while keeping him in position.

The "come" is taught when the dog is on leash and heeling. Simply walk along, then suddenly take a step backward, saying "Come!" Pull the leash as you give the command and the dog will turn and follow you. Continue walking backward, repeatedly saying "Come," and tightening the leash if necessary.

Once the dog has mastered the exercises while on leash, try taking the leash off and going through the same routine, beginning with the heeling exercise. If the dog doesn't respond promptly, he needs review with the leash on. But patience and persistence will be rewarded, for you will have a dog you can trust to respond promptly under all conditions.

Even after they are well trained, dogs sometimes develop bad habits that are hard to break. Jumping on people is a common habit, and all members of the family must assist if it is to be broken. If the dog is a large or medium breed, take a step forward and raise your knee just as he starts to jump on you. As your knee strikes the dog's chest, command "Down!" in a scolding voice. When a small dog jumps on you, take both front paws in your hands, and, while talking in a pleasant tone of voice, step on the dog's back feet just hard enough to hurt them slightly. With either method the dog is taken by surprise and doesn't associate the discomfort with the person causing it.

Occasionally a dog may be too chummy with guests who don't care for dogs. If the dog has had obedience training, simply command "Come!" When he responds, have him sit beside you.

Excessive barking is likely to bring complaints from neighbors, and persistent efforts may be needed to subdue a dog that barks without provocation. To correct the habit, you must be close to the dog when he starts barking. Encircle his muzzle with both hands, hold his mouth shut, and command "Quiet!" in a firm voice. He should soon learn to respond so you can control him simply by giving the command.

Sniffing other dogs is an annoying habit. If the dog is off leash and sniffs other dogs, ignoring your commands to come, he needs

Benching area at Westminster Kennel Club Show.

to review the lessons on basic behavior. When the dog is on leash
scold him, then pull on the leash, command "Heel," and wal
away from the other dog.

A well-trained dog will be no problem if you decide to take hir
with you when you travel. No matter how well he responds, how
ever, he should never be permitted off leash when you walk him i
a strange area. Distractions will be more tempting, and there wi
be more chance of his being attacked by other dogs. So wheneve
the dog travels with you, take his leash along—and use it.

Judging for Best in Show at Westminster Kennel Club Show.

Show Competition

Centuries ago, it was common practice to hold agricultural fairs in conjunction with spring and fall religious festivals, and to these gatherings, cattle, dogs, and other livestock were brought for exchange. As time went on, it became customary to provide entertainment, too. Dogs often participated in such sporting events as bull baiting, bear baiting, and ratting. Then the dog that exhibited the greatest skill in the arena was also the one that brought the highest price when time came for barter or sale. Today, these fairs seem a far cry from our highly organized bench shows and field trials. But they were the forerunners of modern dog shows and played an important role in shaping the development of purebred dogs.

The first organized dog show was held at Newcastle, England, in 1859. Later that same year, a show was held at Birmingham. At both shows dogs were divided into four classes and only Pointers and Setters were entered. In 1860, the first dog show in Germany was held at Apoldo, where nearly one hundred dogs were exhibited and entries were divided into six groups. Interest expanded rapidly, and by the time the Paris Exhibition was held in 1878, the dog show was a fixture of international importance.

In the United States, the first organized bench show was held in 1874 in conjunction with the meeting of the Illinois State Sportsmen's Association in Chicago, and all entries were dogs of sporting breeds. Although the show was a rather casual affair, interest spread quickly. Before the end of the year, shows were held in Oswego, New York, Mineola, Long Island, and Memphis, Tennessee. And the latter combined a bench show with the first organized field trial ever held in the United States. In January 1875, an all-breed show (the first in the United States) was held at Detroit, Michigan. From then on, interest increased rapidly, though rules were not always uniform, for there was no organization through which to coordinate activities until September 1884 when The American Kennel Club was founded. Now the largest dog

137

registing organization in the world, the AKC is an association of several hundred member clubs—all breed, specialty, field trial, and obedience groups—each represented by a delegate to the AKC.

The several thousand shows and trials held annually in the United States do much to stimulate interest in breeding to produce better looking, sounder, purebred dogs. For breeders, shows provide a means of measuring the merits of their work as compared with accomplishments of other breeders. For hundreds of thousands of dog fanciers, they provide an absorbing hobby.

Bench Shows

At bench (or conformation) shows, dogs are rated comparatively on their physical qualities (or conformation) in accordance with breed Standards which have been approved by The American Kennel Club. Characteristics such as size, coat, color, placement of eye or ear, general soundness, etc., are the basis for selecting the best dog in a class. Only purebred dogs are eligible to compete and if the show is one where points toward a championship are to be awarded, a dog must be at least six months old.

Bench shows are of various types. An all-breed show has classes for all of the breeds recognized by The American Kennel Club as well as a Miscellaneous Class for breeds not recognized, such as the Australian Cattle Dog, the Ibizan Hound, the Spinoni Italiani, etc. A sanctioned match is an informal meeting where dogs compete but not for championship points. A specialty show is confined to a single breed. Other shows may restrict entries to champions of record, to American-bred dogs, etc. Competition for Junior Showmanship or for Best Brace, Best Team, or Best Local Dog may be included. Also, obedience competition is held in conjunction with many bench shows.

The term "bench show" is somewhat confusing in that shows of this type may be either "benched" or "unbenched." At the former, each dog is assigned an individual numbered stall where he must remain throughout the show except for times when he is being judged, groomed, or exercised. At unbenched shows, no stalls are provided and dogs are kept in their owners' cars or in crates when not being judged.

A show where a dog is judged for conformation actually constitutes an elimination contest. To begin with, the dogs of a single breed compete with others of their breed in one of the regular classes: Puppy, Novice, Bred by Exhibitor, American-Bred, or

138

Open, and, finally, Winners, where the top dogs of the preceding five classes meet. The next step is the judging for Best of Breed (or Best of Variety of Breed). Here the Winners Dog and Winners Bitch (or the dog named Winners if only one prize is awarded) compete with any champions that are entered, together with any undefeated dogs that have competed in additional non-regular classes. The dog named Best of Breed (or Best of Variety of Breed), then goes on to compete with the other Best of Breed winners in his Group. The dogs that win in Group competition then compete for the final and highest honor, Best in Show.

When the Winners Class is divided by sex, championship points are awarded the Winners Dog and Winners Bitch. If the Winners Class is not divided by sex, championship points are awarded the dog or bitch named Winners. The number of points awarded varies, depending upon such factors as the number of dogs competing, the Schedule of Points established by the Board of Directors of the AKC, and whether the dog goes on to win Best of Breed, the Group, and Best in Show.

In order to become a champion, a dog must win fifteen points, including points from at least two major wins—that is, at least two shows where three or more points are awarded. The major wins must be under two different judges, and one or more of the remaining points must be won under a third judge. The most points ever awarded at a show is five and the least is one, so, in order to become a champion, a dog must be exhibited and win in at least three shows, and usually he is shown many times before he wins his championship.

Pure Bred Dogs—American Kennel Gazette and other dog magazines contain lists of forthcoming shows, together with names and addresses of sponsoring organizations to which you may write for entry forms and information relative to fees, closing dates, etc. Before entering your dog in a show for the first time, you should familiarize yourself with the regulations and rules governing competition. You may secure such information from The American Kennel Club or from a local dog club specializing in your breed. It is essential that you also familiarize yourself with the AKC approved Standard for your breed so you will be fully aware of characteristics worthy of merit as well as those considered faulty, or possibly even serious enough to disqualify the dog from competition. For instance, monorchidism (failure of one testicle to descend) and cryptorchidism (failure of both testicles to descend) are disqualifying faults in all breeds.

If possible, you should first attend a show as a spectator and observe judging procedures from ringside. It will also be helpful to join a local breed club and to participate in sanctioned matches before entering an all-breed show.

The dog should be equipped with a narrow leather show lead and a show collar—never an ornamented or spiked collar. For benched shows, either a bench crate or a metal-link bench chain to fasten the dog to the bench will be needed. For unbenched shows, the dog's crate should be taken along so that he may be confined in comfort when he is not appearing in the ring. A dog should never be left in a car with all the windows closed. In hot weather the temperature will become unbearable in a very short time. Heat exhaustion may result from even a short period of confinement, and death may ensue.

Food and water dishes will be needed, as well as a supply of the food and water to which the dog is accustomed. Brushes and combs are also necessary, so that you may give the dog's coat a final grooming after you arrive at the show.

Familiarize yourself with the schedule of classes ahead of time, for the dog must be fed and exercised and permitted to relieve himself, and any last-minute grooming completed before his class is called. Both you and the dog should be ready to enter the ring unhurriedly. A good deal of skill in conditioning, training, and handling is required if a dog is to be presented properly. And it is essential that the handler himself be composed, for a jittery handler will transmit his nervousness to his dog.

Once the class is assembled in the ring, the judge will ask that the dogs be paraded in line, moving counter-clockwise in a circle. If you have trained your dog well, you will have no difficulty controlling him in the ring, where he must change pace quickly and gracefully and walk and trot elegantly and proudly with head erect. The show dog must also stand quietly for inspection, posing like a statue for several minutes while the judge observes his structure in detail, examines teeth, feet, coat, etc. When the judge calls your dog forward for individual inspection, do not attempt to converse, but answer any questions he may ask.

As the judge examines the class, he measures each dog against the ideal described in the Standard, then measures the dogs against each other in a comparative sense and selects for first place the dog that comes closest to conforming to the Standard for its breed. If your dog isn't among the winners, don't grumble. If he places first, don't brag loudly. For a bad loser is disgusting, but a poor winner is insufferable.

Junior Showmanship Competition at Westminster Kennel Club Show.

Bench crate.   Wagon crate.

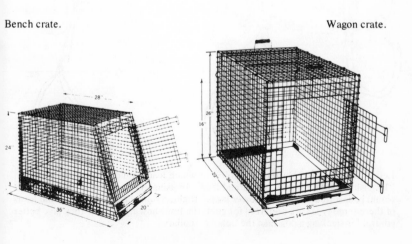

Collars. At the top are two "pinch" or "spiked" collars that are not permitted in AKC shows. Below are two permissible "choke" collars, the one on the right of steel chain and the one on the left of braided nylon. While the choke collars are permitted in conformation shows, they are used more often in obedience competition.

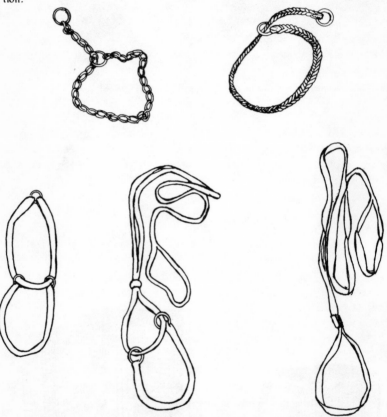

Left, "English" or "Martingale" collar to which lead would be attached. Center, "English" or "Martingale" collar and lead. In using either of these, the dog's head would be inserted through the lower loop. Right, nylon slip lead. Collars and leads of these three types are preferred for conformation showing because they give better control for stacking a dog than the "choke" collars.

Obedience Competition

For hundreds of years, dogs have been used in England and Germany in connection with police and guard work, and their working potential has been evaluated through tests devised to show agility, strength, and courage. Organized training has also been popular with English and German breeders for many years, although it was first practiced primarily for the purpose of training large breeds in aggressive tactics.

There was little interest in obedience training in the United States until 1933 when Mrs. Whitehouse Walker returned from England and enthusiastically introduced the sport. Two years later, Mrs. Walker persuaded The American Kennel Club to approve organized obedience activities and to assume jurisdiction over obedience rules. Since then, interest has increased at a phenomenal rate, for obedience competition is not only a sport the average spectator can follow readily, but also a sport for which the average owner can train his own dog easily. Obedience competition is suitable for all breeds. Furthermore, there is no limit to the number of dogs that may win in competition, for each dog is scored individually on the basis of a point rating system.

The dog is judged on his response to certain commands, and if he gains a high enough score in three successive trials under different judges, he wins an obedience degree. Degrees awarded are "CD"—Companion Dog; "CDX"—Companion Dog Excellent; and "UD"—Utility Dog. A fourth degree, the "TD" or Tracking Dog degree, may be won at any time and tests for it are held apart from dog shows. The qualifying score is a minimum of 170 points out of a possible total of 200, with no score in any one exercise less than 50% of the points allotted.

Since obedience titles are progressive, earlier titles (with the exception of the tracking degree) are dropped as a dog acquires the next higher degree. If an obedience title is gained in another country in addition to the United States, that fact is signified by the word "International," followed by the title.

Trials for obedience trained dogs are held at most of the larger bench shows, and obedience training clubs are to be found in almost all communities today. Information concerning forthcoming trials and lists of obedience training clubs are included regularly in *Pure Bred Dogs–American Kennel Gazette*—and other dog magazines. Pamphlets containing rules and regulations governing obedience competition are available upon request from The American Kennel Club, 51 Madison Avenue, New York, N.Y. 10010. Rules are revised occasionally, so if you are interested in participating in obedience competition, you should be sure your copy of the regulations is current.

All dogs must comply with the same rules, although in broad jump, high jump, and bar jump competition, the jumps are adjusted to the size of the breed. Classes at obedience trials are divided into Novice (A and B), Open (A and B), and Utility (which may be divided into A and B, at the option of the sponsoring club and with the approval of The American Kennel Club).

The Novice class is for dogs that have not won the title Companion Dog. In Novice A, no person who has previously handled a dog that has won a CD title in the obedience ring at a licensed or member trial, and no person who has regularly trained such a dog, may enter or handle a dog. The handler must be the dog's owner or a member of the owner's immediate family. In Novice B, dogs may be handled by the owner or any other person.

The Open A class is for dogs that have won the CD title but have not won the CDX title. Obedience judges and licensed handlers may not enter or handle dogs in this class. Each dog must be handled by the owner or by a member of his immediate family. The Open B class is for dogs that have won the title CD or CDX. A dog may continue to compete in this class after it has won the title UD. Dogs in this class may be handled by the owner or any other person.

The Utility class is for dogs that have won the title CDX. Dogs that have won the title UD may continue to compete in this class, and dogs may be handled by the owner or any other person. Provided the AKC approves, a club may choose to divide the Utility class into Utility A and Utility B. When this is done, the Utility A class is for dogs that have won the title CDX and have not won the title UD. Obedience judges and licensed handlers may not enter or handle dogs in this class. All other dogs that are eligible for the Utility class but not eligible for Utility A may be entered in Utility B.

Novice competition includes such exercises as heeling on and off lead, the stand for examination, coming on recall, and the long sit and the long down.

In Open competition, the dog must perform such exercises as heeling free, the drop on recall, and the retrieve on the flat and over the high jump. Also, he must execute the broad jump, and the long sit and long down.

Bar Jump.

In the Utility class, competition includes scent discrimination, the directed retrieve, the signal exercise, directed jumping, and the group examination.

Tracking is the most difficult test. It is always done out-of-doors, of course, and, for obvious reasons, cannot be held at a dog show. The dog must follow a scent trail that is about a quarter mile in length. He is also required to find a scent object (glove, wallet, or other article) left by a stranger who has walked the course to lay down the scent. The dog is required to follow the trail a half to two hours after the scent is laid.

An ideal way to train a dog for obedience competition is to join an obedience class or a training club. In organized class work, beginners' classes cover pretty much the same exercises as those described in the chapter on manners. However, through class work you will develop greater precision than is possible in training your dog by yourself. Amateur handlers often cause the dog to be penalized, for if the handler fails to abide by the rules, it is the dog that suffers the penalty. A common infraction of the rules is using more than one signal or command where regulations stipulate only one may be used. Classwork will help eliminate such errors, which the owner may make unconsciously if he is working alone. Working with a class will also acquaint both dog and handler with ring procedure so that obedience trials will not present unforeseen problems.

Thirty or forty owners and dogs often comprise a class, and exercises are performed in unison, with individual instruction provided if it is required. The procedure followed in training—in fact, even wording of various commands—may vary from instructor to instructor. Equipment used will vary somewhat, also, but will usually include a training collar and leash, a long line, a dumbbell, and a jumping stick. The latter may be a short length of heavy doweling or a broom handle and both it and the dumbbell are usually painted white for increased visibility.

A bitch in season must never be taken to a training class, so before enrolling a female dog, you should determine whether she may be expected to come into season before classes are scheduled to end. If you think she will, it is better to wait and enroll her in a later course, rather than start the course and then miss classes for several weeks.

In addition to the time devoted to actual work in class, the dog must have regular, daily training sessions for practice at home. Before each class or home training session, the dog should be exercised so he will not be highly excited when the session starts, and he must be given an opportunity to relieve himself before the session begins. (Should he have an accident during the class, it is your responsibility to clean up after him.) The dog should be fed several hours before time for the class to begin or else after the class is over—never just before going to class.

If you decide to enter your dog in obedience competition, it is well to enter a small, informal show the first time. Dogs are usually called in the order in which their names appear in the catalog, so as soon as you arrive at the show, acquaint yourself with the schedule. If your dog is not the first to be judged, spend some time at ringside, observing the routine so you will know what to expect when your dog's turn comes.

In addition to collar, leash, and other equipment, you should take your dog's food and water pans and a supply of the food and water to which he is accustomed. You should also take his brushes and combs in order to give him a last-minute brushing before you enter the ring. It is important that the dog look his best even though he isn't to be judged on his appearance.

Before entering the ring, exercise your dog, give him a drink of water, and permit him to relieve himself. Once your dog enters the ring, give him your full attention and be sure to give voice commands distinctly so he will hear and understand, for there will be many distractions at ringside.

Dumbbells.

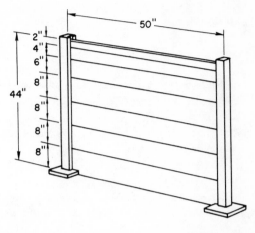

50"

2"
4"
6"
8"
8"
8"
8"

44"

Solid hurdle.

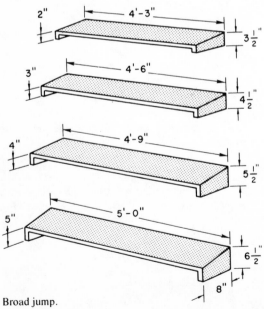

2"

4'-3"

$3\frac{1}{2}$"

3"

4'-6"

$4\frac{1}{2}$"

4"

4'-9"

$5\frac{1}{2}$"

5"

5'-0"

$6\frac{1}{2}$"

8"

Broad jump.

Top dogs in Utility Class. This illustrates the variety of breeds that compete in obedience.

Genetics

Genetics, the science of heredity, deals with the processes by which physical and mental traits of parents are transmitted to offspring. For centuries, man has been trying to solve these puzzles, but only in the last two hundred years has significant progress been made.

During the eighteenth century, Kölreuter, a German scientist, made revolutionary discoveries concerning plant sexuality and hybridization but was unable to explain just how hereditary processes worked. In the middle of the nineteenth century, Gregor Johann Mendel, an Augustinian monk, experimented with the ordinary garden pea and made other discoveries of major significance. He found that an inherited characteristic was inherited as a complete unit, and that certain characteristics predominated over others. Next, he observed that the hereditary characteristics of each parent are contained in each offspring, even when they are not visible, and that "hidden" characteristics can be transferred without change in their nature to the grandchildren, or even later generations. Finally, he concluded that although heredity contains an element of uncertainty, some things are predictable on the basis of well-defined mathematical laws.

Unfortunately, Mendel's published paper went unheeded, and when he died in 1884 he was still virtually unknown to the scientific world. But other researchers were making discoveries, too. In 1900, three different scientists reported to learned societies that much of their research in hereditary principles had been proved years before by Gregor Mendel and that findings matched perfectly.

Thus, hereditary traits were proved to be transmitted through the chromosomes found in pairs in every living being, one of each pair contributed by the mother, the other by the father. Within each chromosome have been found hundreds of smaller structures, or genes, which are the actual determinants of hereditary characteristics. Some genes are dominant and will be seen in the offspring. Others are recessive and will not be outwardly apparent, yet can be passed on to the offspring to combine with a similar recessive gene of the other parent and thus be seen. Or they may be passed on to the offspring, not be outwardly apparent, but be passed on again to become apparent in a later generation.

Once the genetic theory of inheritance became widely known, scientists began drawing a well-defined line between inheritance and environment. More recent studies show some overlapping of these influences and indicate a combination of the two may be responsible for certain characteristics. For instance, studies have proved that extreme cold increases the amount of black pigment in the skin and hair of the "Himalayan" rabbit, although it has little or no effect on the white or colored rabbit. Current research also indicates that even though characteristics are determined by the genes, some environmental stress occurring at a particular period of pregnancy might cause physical change in the embryo.

Long before breeders had any knowledge of genetics, they practiced one of its most important principles—selective breeding. Experience quickly showed that "like begets like," and by breeding like with like and discarding unlike offspring, the various individual breeds were developed to the point where variations were relatively few. Selective breeding is based on the idea of maintaining the quality of a breed at the highest possible level, while improving whatever defects are prevalent. It requires that only the top dogs in a litter be kept for later breeding, and that inferior specimens be ruthlessly eliminated.

In planning any breeding program, the first requisite is a definite goal—that is, to have clearly in mind a definite picture of the type of dog you wish eventually to produce. To attempt to breed perfection is to approach the problem unrealistically. But if you don't breed for improvement, it is preferable that you not breed at all.

As a first step, you should select a bitch that exemplifies as many of the desired characteristics as possible and mate her with a dog that also has as many of the desired characteristics as possible. If you start with mediocre pets, you will produce mediocre pet puppies. If you decide to start with more than one bitch, all should closely approach the type you desire, since you will then stand a better chance of producing uniformly good puppies from all. Breeders often start with a single bitch and keep the best bitches in every succeeding generation.

Experienced breeders look for "prepotency" in breeding stock—that is, the ability of a dog or bitch to transmit traits to most or all of its offspring. While the term is usually used to describe the transmission of good qualities, a dog may also be prepotent in

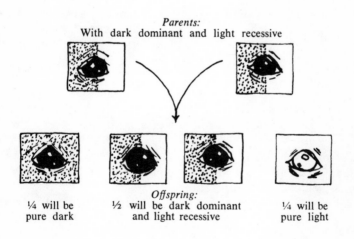

Parents:
One pure dark eyes
and one pure light eyes

Dark eyes   Light eyes

Offspring:
Eyes dark (dominant) with light recessive

Parents:
With dark dominant and light recessive

¼ will be   ½ will be dark dominant   ¼ will be
pure dark   and light recessive   pure light

Offspring:

The above is a schematic representation of the Mendelian law as it applies to the inheritance of eye color. The law applies in the same way to the inheritance of other physical characteristics.

transmitting faults. To be prepotent in a practical sense, a dog must possess many characteristics controlled by dominant genes. If desired characteristics are recessive, they will be apparent in the offspring only if carried by both sire and dam. Prepotent dogs and bitches usually come from a line of prepotent ancestors, but the mere fact that a dog has exceptional ancestors will not necessarily mean that he himself will produce exceptional offspring.

A single dog may sire a tremendous number of puppies, whereas a bitch can produce only a comparatively few litters during her lifetime. Thus, a sire's influence may be very widespread as compared to that of a bitch. But in evaluating a particular litter, it must be remembered that the bitch has had as much influence as has had the dog.

Inbreeding, line-breeding, outcrossing, or a combination of the three are the methods commonly used in selective breeding.

Inbreeding is the mating together of closely related animals, such as father-daughter, mother-son, or brother-sister. Although some breeders insist such breeding will lead to the production of defective individuals, it is through rigid inbreeding that all breeds of dogs have been established. Controlled tests have shown that any harmful effects appear within the first five or ten generations, and that if rigid selection is exercised from the beginning, a vigorous inbred strain will be built up.

Line-breeding is also the mating together of individuals related by family lines. However, matings are made not so much on the basis of the dog's and bitch's relationship to each other, but, instead, on the basis of their relationship to a highly admired ancestor, with a view to perpetuating that ancestor's qualities. Line-breeding constitutes a long-range program and cannot be accomplished in a single generation.

Outcrossing is the breeding together of two dogs that are unrelated in family lines. Actually, since breeds have been developed through the mating of close relatives, all dogs within any given breed are related to some extent. There are few breedings that are true outcrosses, but if there is no common ancestor within five generations, a mating is usually considered an outcross.

Experienced breeders sometimes outcross for one generation in order to eliminate a particular fault, then go back to inbreeding or line-breeding. Neither the good effects nor the bad effects of outcrossing can be truly evaluated in a single mating, for undesirable recessive traits may be introduced into a strain, yet not show up for several generations. Outcrossing is better left to experienced breeders, for continual outcrossing results in a wide variation in type and great uncertainty as to the results that may be expected.

Two serious defects that are believed heritable—subluxation and orchidism—should be zealously guarded against, and afflicted dogs and their offspring should be eliminated from breeding programs. Subluxation is a condition of the hip joint where the bone of the socket is eroded and the head of the thigh bone is also worn away, causing lameness which becomes progressively more serious until the dog is unable to walk. Orchidism is the failure of one or both testicles to develop and descend properly. When one testicle is involved, the term "monorchid" is used. When both are involved, "cryptorchid" is used. A cryptorchid is almost always sterile, whereas a monorchid is usually fertile. There is evidence that orchidism "runs in families" and that a monorchid transmits the tendency through bitch and male puppies alike.

Through the years, many misconceptions concerning heredity have been perpetuated. Perhaps the one most widely perpetuated is the idea evolved hundreds of years ago that somehow characteristics were passed on through the mixing of the blood of the parents. We still use terminology evolved from that theory when we speak of bloodlines, or describe individuals as full-blooded, despite the fact that the theory was disproved more than a century ago.

Also inaccurate and misleading is any statement that a definite fraction or proportion of an animal's inherited characteristics can be positively attributed to a particular ancestor. Individuals lacking knowledge of genetics sometimes declare that an individual receives half his inherited characteristics from each parent, a quarter from each grandparent, an eighth from each great-grandparent, etc. Thousands of volumes of scientific findings have been published, but no simple way has been found to determine positively which characteristics have been inherited from which ancestors, for the science of heredity is infinitely complex.

Any breeder interested in starting a serious breeding program should study several of the books on canine genetics and breeding and whelping that are currently available. Two excellent works covering these subjects are *Meisen Breeding Manual,* by Hilda Meisenzahl, and *The Standard Book of Dog Breeding,* by Dr. Alvin Grossman—both published by the publisher of this book.

Whelping box. Detail at right shows proper side-wall construction which helps keep small puppies confined and provides sheltered nook to prevent crushing or smothering.

Breeding and Whelping

The breeding life of a bitch begins when she comes into season the first time at the age of eight to ten months. Thereafter, she will come in season at roughly six-month intervals. Her maximum fertility builds up from puberty to full maturity and then declines until a state of total sterility is reached in old age. Just when this occurs is hard to determine, for the fact that an older bitch shows signs of being in season doesn't necessarily mean she is still capable of reproducing.

The length of the season varies from eighteen to twenty-one days. The first indication is a pronounced swelling of the vulva with coincidental bleeding (called "showing color") for about the first seven to nine days. The discharge gradually turns to a creamy color, and it is during this phase (estrus), from about the tenth to the fifteenth days, that the bitch is ovulating and is receptive to the male. The ripe, unfertilized ova survive for about seventy-two hours. If fertilization doesn't occur, the ova die and are discharged the next time the bitch comes in season. If fertilization does take place, each ovum attaches itself to the walls of the uterus, a membrane forms to seal it off, and a foetus develops from it.

Following the estrus phase, the bitch is still in season until about the twenty-first day and will continue to be attractive to males, although she will usually fight them off as she did the first few days. Nevertheless, to avoid accidental mating, the bitch must be confined for the entire period. Virtual imprisonment is necessary, for male dogs display uncanny abilities in their efforts to reach a bitch in season.

The odor that attracts the males is present in the bitch's urine, so it is advisable to take her a good distance from the house before permitting her to relieve herself. To eliminate problems completely, your veterinarian can prescribe a preparation that will disguise the odor but will not interfere with breeding when the time is right. Many fanciers use such preparations when exhibiting a bitch and find that nearby males show no interest whatsoever. But it is not advisable to permit a bitch to run loose when she has been given a product of this type, for during estrus she will seek the company of male dogs and an accidental mating may occur.

A potential brood bitch, regardless of breed, should have good bone, ample breadth and depth of ribbing, and adequate room in the pelvic region. Unless a bitch is physically mature—well beyond the puppy stage when she has her first season—breeding should be delayed until her second or a later season. Furthermore, even though it is possible for a bitch to conceive twice a year, she should not be bred oftener than once a year. A bitch that is bred too often will age prematurely and her puppies are likely to lack vigor.

Two or three months before a bitch is to be mated, her physical condition should be considered carefully. If she is too thin, provide a rich, balanced diet plus the regular exercise needed to develop strong, supple muscles. Daily exercise on the lead is as necessary for the too-thin bitch as for the too-fat one, although the latter will need more exercise and at a brisker pace, as well as a reduction of food, if she is to be brought to optimum condition. A prospective brood bitch must have had permanent distemper shots as well as rabies vaccination. And a month before her season is due, a veterinarian should examine a stool specimen for worms. If there is evidence of infestation, the bitch should be wormed.

A dog may be used at stud from the time he reaches physical maturity, well on into old age. The first time your bitch is bred, it is well to use a stud that has already proven his ability by having sired other litters. The fact that a neighbor's dog is readily available should not influence your choice, for to produce the best puppies, you must select the stud most suitable from a genetic standpoint.

If the stud you prefer is not going to be available at the time your bitch is to be in season, you may wish to consult your veterinarian concerning medications available for inhibiting the onset of the season. With such preparations, the bitch's season can be delayed indefinitely.

Usually the first service will be successful. However, if it isn't, in most cases an additional service is given free, provided the stud dog is still in the possession of the same owner. If the bitch misses, it may be because her cycle varies widely from normal. Through microscopic examination, a veterinarian can determine exactly when the bitch is entering the estrus phase and thus is likely to conceive.

The owner of the stud should give you a stud-service certificate, providing a four-generation pedigree for the sire and showing the date of mating. The litter registration application is completed only after the puppies are whelped, but it, too, must be signed by the owner of the stud as well as the owner of the bitch. Registration forms may be secured by writing The American Kennel Club.

In normal pregnancy there is visible enlargement of the abdomen by the end of the fifth week. By palpation (feeling with the fingers) a veterinarian may be able to distinguish developing puppies as early as three weeks after mating, but it is unwise for a novice to poke and prod, and try to detect the presence of unborn puppies.

The gestation period normally lasts nine weeks, although it may vary from sixty-one to sixty-five days. If it goes beyond sixty-five days from the date of mating, a veterinarian should be consulted.

During the first four or five weeks, the bitch should be permitted her normal amount of activity. As she becomes heavier, she should be walked on the lead, but strenuous running and jumping should be avoided. Her diet should be well balanced (see page 41), and if she should become constipated, small amounts of mineral oil may be added to her food.

A whelping box should be secured about two weeks before the puppies are due, and the bitch should start then to use it as her bed so she will be accustomed to it by the time puppies arrive. Preferably, the box should be square, with each side long enough so that the bitch can stretch out full length and have several inches to spare at either end. The bottom should be padded with an old cotton rug or other material that is easily laundered. Edges of the padding should be tacked to the floor of the box so the puppies will not get caught in it and smother. Once it is obvious labor is about to begin, the padding should be covered with several layers of spread-out newspapers. Then, as papers become soiled, the top layer can be pulled off, leaving the area clean.

Forty-eight to seventy-two hours before the litter is to be whelped, a definite change in the shape of the abdomen will be noted. Instead of looking barrel-shaped, the abdomen will sag pendulously. Breasts usually redden and become enlarged, and milk may be present a day or two before the puppies are whelped. As the time becomes imminent, the bitch will probably scratch and root at her bedding in an effort to make a nest, and will refuse food and ask to be let out every few minutes. But the surest sign is a drop in temperature of two or three degrees about twelve hours before labor begins.

The bitch's abdomen and flanks will contract sharply when labor actually starts, and for a few minutes she will attempt to expel a puppy, then rest for a while and try again. Someone should stay with the bitch the entire time whelping is taking place, and if she appears to be having unusual difficulties, a veterinarian should be called.

Puppies are usually born head first, though some may be born feet first and no difficulty encountered. Each puppy is enclosed in a separate membranous sac that the bitch will remove with her teeth. She will sever the umbilical cord, which will be attached to the soft, spongy afterbirth that is expelled right after the puppy emerges. Usually the bitch eats the afterbirth, so it is necessary to watch and make sure one is expelled for each puppy whelped. If afterbirth is retained, the bitch may develop peritonitis and die.

The dam will lick and nuzzle each newborn puppy until it is warm and dry and ready to nurse. If puppies arrive so close together that she can't take care of them, you can help her by rubbing the puppies dry with a soft cloth. If several have been whelped but the bitch continues to be in labor, all but one should be removed and placed in a small box lined with clean towels and warmed to about seventy degrees. The bitch will be calmer if one puppy is left with her at all times.

Whelping sometimes continues as long as twenty-four hours for a very large litter, but a litter of two or three puppies may be whelped in an hour. When the bitch settles down, curls around the puppies and nuzzles them to her, it usually indicates that all have been whelped.

The bitch should be taken away for a few minutes while you clean the box and arrange clean padding. If her coat is soiled, sponge it clean before she returns to the puppies. Once she is back in the box, offer her a bowl of warm beef broth and a pan of cool water, placing both where she will not have to get up in order to reach them. As soon as she indicates interest in food, give her a generous bowl of chopped meat to which codliver oil and dicalcium phosphate have been added.

If inadequate amounts of calcium are provided during the period the puppies are nursing, eclampsia may develop. Symptoms are violent trembling, rapid rise in temperature, and rigidity of muscles. Veterinary assistance must be secured immediately, for death may result in a very short time. Treatment consists of massive doses of calcium gluconate administered intravenously, after which symptoms subside in a miraculously short time.

For weak or very small puppies, supplemental feeding is often recommended. Any one of three different methods may be used: tube-feeding (with a catheter attached to a syringe), using an eye-dropper (this method requires great care in order to avoid getting formula in the lungs), or using a tiny bottle (the "pet nurser" available at most pet supply stores). The commercially prepared puppy formulas are most convenient and are readily obtainable from a veterinarian, who can also tell you which method of administering the formula is most practical in your particular case. It is important to remember that equipment must be kept scrupulously clean. It can be sterilized by boiling, or it may be soaked in a Clorox solution, then washed carefully and dried between feedings.

All puppies are born blind and their eyes open when they are ten to fourteen days old. At first the eyes have a bluish cast and appear weak, and the puppies must be protected from strong light until at least ten days after the eyes open.

To ensure proper emotional development, young dogs should be shielded from loud noises and rough handling. Being lifted by the front legs is painful and may result in permanent injury to the shoulders. So when lifting a puppy, always place one hand under the chest with the forefinger between the front legs, and place the other hand under his bottom.

Flannelized rubber sheeting is an ideal surface for the bottom of the bed for the new puppies. It is inexpensive and washable, and will provide a surface that will give the puppies traction so that they will not slip either while nursing or when learning to walk.

Sometimes the puppies' nails are so long and sharp that they scratch the bitch's breasts. Since the nails are soft, they can be trimmed with ordinary scissors.

At about four weeks of age, formula should be provided. The amount fed each day should be increased over a period of two weeks, when the puppies can be weaned completely. One of the commercially prepared formulas can be mixed according to directions on the container, or formula can be prepared at home in accordance with instructions from a veterinarian. The formula should be warmed to lukewarm, and poured into a shallow pan placed on the floor of the box. After his mouth has been dipped into the mixture a few times, a puppy will usually start to lap formula. All puppies should be allowed to eat from the same pan, but be sure the small ones get their share. If they are pushed aside, feed them separately. Permit the puppies to nurse part of the time, but gradually increase the number of meals of formula. By the time the puppies are five weeks old, the dam should be allowed with them only at night. When they are about six weeks old, they should be weaned completely. Three meals a day are usually sufficient from this time until the puppies are about three months old, when feedings are reduced to two a day. About the time the dog reaches one year of age, feedings may be reduced to one each day. (For further information on this subject, see page 38.)

Once they are weaned, puppies should be given temporary distemper injections every two weeks until they are old enough for permanent inoculations. At six weeks, stool specimens should be checked for worms, for almost without exception, puppies become infested. Specimens should be checked again at eight weeks, and as often thereafter as your veterinarian recommends.

Sometimes owners decide as a matter of convenience to have a bitch spayed or a male castrated. While this is recommended when a dog has a serious inheritable defect or when abnormalities of reproductive organs develop, in sound, normal purebred dogs, spaying a bitch or castrating a male may prove a definite disadvantage. The operations automatically bar dogs from competing in shows as well as precluding use for breeding. The operations are seldom dangerous, but they should not be performed without serious consideration of these facts.